SALLY'S BAKING ADDICTION

Irresistible Cookies, Cupcakes & Desserts for Your Sweet-Tooth Fix

First published in 2014 by Race Point Publishing,
an imprint of The Quarto Group,
142 West 36th Street 4th Floor,
New York, NY 10018, USA
(212) 779-4972 **www.Quarto.com**

Race Point Publishing titles are also available at discount for retail, wholesale, promotional, and bulk purchase. For details, contact the Special Sales Manager by email at specialsales@quarto.com or by mail at The Quarto Group, Attn: Special Sales Manager, 100 Cummings Center Suite 265D, Beverly, MA 01915, USA.

ISBN: 978-1-63106-276-6

Library of Congress Cataloging-in-Publication Data

Names: McKenney, Sally, author.
Title: Sally's baking addiction : irresistible cookies, cupcakes, & desserts
   for your sweet-tooth fix / Sally McKenney, sprinkle-lover & founder of
   Sally's Baking Addiction.
Description: New York : Race Point Publishing, [2016] | Includes index.
Identifiers: LCCN 2016025197| ISBN 9781631062766 (pbk.) | ISBN 9781937994341
   (hardcover)
Subjects: LCSH: Desserts. | Cupcakes. | Baking. | Cookies. | LCGFT: Cookbooks.
Classification: LCC TX765 .M435 2016 | DDC 641.86--dc23 LC record available at https://lccn.loc.gov/2016025197

Editorial Director: Jeannine Dillon
Managing Editor: Erin Canning
Project Editor: Jason Chappell
Copyeditor: Helena Caldon
Design: Heidi North

20 19 18 17 16 15 14

Printed in China

SALLY'S BAKING ADDICTION

Irresistible Cookies, Cupcakes, & Desserts for Your Sweet Tooth Fix

Race Point
PUBLISHING

SALLY McKENNEY
Sprinkle Lover & Creator of
SallysBakingAddiction.com

ACKNOWLEDGMENTS

I could not have written this book alone. A huge thank you to my talented and creative editor, Jeannine Dillon, who stumbled upon my blog and loved what she saw. The moment you emailed me changed my life forever. A huge thanks to the rest of the Race Point Publishing team for producing such a wonderful book.

Thank you to all my family, friends, and gracious readers for constantly supporting my baking addiction. I wouldn't have a blog or a book without you!

Thank you to my loving parents and supportive older sisters, Sarah and Saundra. You taught me to celebrate food and have never stopped believing in me. Thank you Mom for the daily reminders to shine my brightest and for teaching me everything I know about gingersnaps. Thank you Dad for sharing my love of carrot cake and for all of the advice as I build my business. Your example taught me to work hard for what I want.

Finally, thank you to my husband, Kevin, for your constant support, encouragement, and emergency trips to the grocery store. You happily listen to me blabber about pie crust and you don't mind living in an apartment cramped with chocolate chips, food props, and light reflectors. And you never complain! It must be all the peanut butter cookies I make for you ....

Grandma Harlett is my baking inspiration.

proud SBA Parents

DEDICATION
To Grandma Harlett,
"garden grandma."
I miss you.

Me, Jude, and Kevin

Before I became a baker, I was a fashionista.

Christmas morning with my sisters. This is normal for us.

Roasting s'mores with my best friend Amy. Amy's favorite dessert is on page 84!

CONTENTS

A BITE OF REAL LIFE FROM SALLY

It's early Saturday morning. I've been holed up in my closet-sized kitchen for hours. There's flour on my face, melted butter splatters on my cabinets, dirty dishes are multiplying, and my recipe notes are nothing more than chicken scratch on chocolate-stained paper.

There's truly nowhere else I'd rather be.

Welcome to my addiction.

I never set out to build a website that regularly receives over six million views per month. My goal when I started *Sally's Baking Addiction* was simply to share the recipes I baked with my friends and family. My mom and fiancé were the only two people to subscribe for the first few months. I remember the day I had 10 page views. Then 100, then 1,000. Within eighteen months, my blog had exploded, and I had to quit my day job working in finance to keep up with it all. *Sally's Baking Addiction* is not just a job or a hobby anymore; it's my life!

I grew up learning that good food can bring loved ones together. We ate homemade bread and lush veggies from my grandma's garden, along with her fresh boysenberry jam. The holidays meant Mom's Gingersnaps (page 117), homemade macaroni and cheese, and pumpkin pie from scratch. Everything I've learned in the kitchen has come from watching others and from years of practice. It took eleven months to perfect my Cake Batter Chocolate Chip Cookies (page 106) and five loaves of Pumpkin Chocolate Chip Bread (page 9) before I stumbled upon the perfect combination of ingredients. That's a lot of chocolate chips! I'm pretty sure I singlehandedly keep Nestle® Toll House® in business.

Familiar ingredients and easy instructions can produce extraordinary food. What makes my kitchen-tested recipes fun to prepare is how uncomplicated they are. There are a million places you need to be each day, and the kitchen isn't necessarily one of them. My goal for this book is to bring you back to the kitchen and show you that baking the perfect vanilla cupcake from scratch is not only delicious, it's also simple and fun—and from the heart. Sprinkles are an added bonus, of course!

I'll be honest, when I was first approached to write this cookbook, I nearly fell out of my chair. Someone wants to put my recipes in a book? Would anyone even want to read it? Then I remembered that I had the same reservations when I began *Sally's Baking Addiction* back in 2011. But it turns out that sharing my recipes, my kitchen mistakes, and my solutions with readers enables me to bring joy to their lives through food, and that is what inspires me to work harder and keep going. After all, I'm a one-woman show—I bake it, I write it, and I shoot it!

The pages of this book are filled with desserts, muffins, cakes, cookies, candies, and more. I even included a substantial chapter dedicated to healthier recipes for those who follow vegan and gluten-free lifestyles. I can't live on peanut butter cups alone! (I can't, right?)

Just a quick note before you get started pursuing your baking addiction: It might help to review some of my baking essentials (such as key ingredients and handy supplies) over the next few pages and see which ones you don't have in your kitchen.

The extra few minutes you spend reading it will probably make baking a little easier.

Whether you are a novice or an experienced baker, I truly hope the recipes on these pages become a permanent part of your repertoire—and I hope you have a sweet tooth!

—*Sally*

SALLY'S KEY INGREDIENTS (UM, PASS THE PEANUT BUTTER, PLEASE!)

BROWN SUGAR: Brown sugar is granulated sugar with a touch of molasses added, making it softer, moister, and more aromatic. Dark brown sugar has more molasses than light brown sugar, but the two may be used interchangeably in my recipes. Just be sure and pack the brown sugar into your measuring cup in all the recipes that call for it.

BUTTER: Most of the recipes in this book that call for butter were tested using unsalted butter. If you substitute salted butter, reduce the salt used in the recipe by ¼ teaspoon per ½ cup of butter. Don't waste your money on fancy expensive butter; I use store-brand all the time.

CHOCOLATE: Some of the recipes in this book call for pure chocolate. There are several different kinds of chocolate: unsweetened; semi-sweet; milk; and white. These chocolates can be sold as chips, chunks, discs, and blocks. When I refer to semi-sweet chocolate or white chocolate in this book, I am referring to baking chocolate, not chocolate chips. I prefer Baker's semi-sweet chocolate and the Ghirardelli white chocolate baking bar. Both are sold as bars in the baking aisle. When I need melted chocolate for a recipe, I use pure chocolate. In some cases, I add a bit of shortening to help thin it out.

When I refer to chocolate chips or white chocolate chips in this book, I mean packaged chocolate chips such as those by Nestle®. Chocolate chips are formulated so that they do not lose their shape when exposed to high heat, so do not use them unless the recipe specifically calls for them. Some recipes in this book require mini chocolate chips or dark chocolate chips, however, regular-sized semi-sweet chocolate chips may be substituted.

COCOA POWDER: There are two types of cocoa powder: natural and Dutch-processed. Most supermarket brands in the US sell natural-style, while Dutch-processed is more typical in Europe. The difference between the two is their alkaline levels and flavor. Dutching cocoa powder gives it a more mellow flavor compared to natural style. For all of the recipes in this book calling for unsweetened cocoa powder, use natural style. I prefer Hershey's® brand.

CONFECTIONERS' SUGAR: Confectioners' sugar is ultra-fine sugar with a smooth and powdery consistency. It is also known as powdered sugar or icing sugar. I prefer to sift powdered sugar when using it in glazes and frostings, though it is not mandatory.

CORNSTARCH: Often sold as "cornflour" outside the US. It is used to thicken dishes and also to prevent caking in powdered sugar. I love it because it softens my cookies, but it is also gluten-free and so is particularly useful when baking for those with celiac disease or those simply following a gluten-free diet.

EGGS: All of the recipes in this book calling for eggs were tested with large eggs. It is imperative to use eggs at room temperature when the recipe specifically calls for it. See page 14

(Jumbo Blueberry Streusel Muffins) for how to bring eggs to room temperature quickly.

GRANULATED SUGAR: Granulated sugar is your everyday, regular, white sugar.

HEAVY CREAM: I like to use heavy cream in glazes and frostings; it provides the creamiest, thickest texture compared to milk or half-and-half (half cream, half milk). Heavy cream (approximately 36% milk fat) may also be sold as whipping cream. Light whipping cream (30% milk fat), or double cream (48% milk fat) may be substituted.

MILK: All of the recipes in this book calling for milk were tested with 1% or unsweetened plain almond milk. However, the following may be substituted: whole milk, 2% milk, soy milk, rice milk, or coconut milk. Buttermilk, known for its tangy flavor and thick texture, is used in some recipes. It tenderizes baked goods and cannot be substituted. There is an easy homemade alternative to buttermilk suggested on page 68.

OATS: I use two types of oats in this cookbook: quick-cooking oats and old-fashioned rolled oats. Quick-cooking oats (also known as quick oats) are more finely ground whole oats, so are more powdery than old-fashioned rolled oats. It's important to use the specific oats called for in the recipe. Rather than always having two kinds of oats in my pantry, I simply have a canister of old-fashioned rolled oats (also known as

SALLY'S KITCHEN ESSENTIALS

whole oats). When I need quick oats for a recipe, I pulse the whole oats in a food processor for about 3 seconds. I prefer Quaker brand oats. Gluten-free recipes in the Healthy Choices chapter use certified gluten-free oats.

OIL: All of the recipes in this book calling for oil were tested with vegetable oil. Canola oil or melted coconut oil may be used instead.

PEANUT BUTTER: All of the recipes in this book calling for peanut butter were tested with Jif® Creamy Peanut Butter, Jif® Crunchy Peanut Butter, or Skippy® Natural-Style Peanut Butter. It's important to use non-runny peanut butter in my recipes to obtain the proper texture and taste (with the exception of Pretzel Peanut Butter Cups, page 88). Homemade peanut butter, which is typically runny and oily, is not ideal for my recipes.

Remember: As with any recipe, if you vary ingredients or make substitutions, the results will likely not be the same.

The recipes in this book were made with everyday kitchen equipment. Here's what you'll need to put these sweet treats on the table:

- two large baking sheets
- two Silicone baking mats (such as Silpat)
- two 12-count muffin pans
- 6-count jumbo muffin pan
- 6-count donut pan
- mini muffin pan
- aluminum foil
- 8 x 8-in (20 x 20cm) or 9 x 9in (23 x 23cm) square baking pan
- 8 x 8-in (20 x 20cm) or 9 x 9in (23 x 23cm) springform pan
- 9 x 5-in (23 x 13cm) loaf pan
- 9 x 13-in (23 x 33cm) baking pan
- 11 x 7-in (28 x 18cm) baking pan
- three 9 x 2-in (23 x 5cm) round cake pans
- sifter
- food processor
- high-speed blender
- electric handheld and/or stand mixer with paddle and whisk attachments

- large, very sharp knife
- small, sharp paring knife
- rubber spatulas
- classic spatula
- small, medium, and large mixing bowls
- measuring cups and spoons
- large cookie scoop
- cooling rack(s)
- cutting board
- oven thermometer
- rolling pin
- wire whisk
- zester
- non-stick cooking spray (such as PAM®)
- rinsed plastic condiment bottle for drizzling
- pastry brush
- small and large frying (skillet) pans

BREADS & MUFFINS

Growing up, my mom enjoyed the quiet early moments of the day while the rest of us snoozed away upstairs. We'd wake up to the smells of chocolate or blueberry muffins, pumpkin bread, and clean laundry. Like my mom, I enjoy working in the peaceful moments before the rest of the world is awake. I use that "me time" for exercise, catching up on emails, and, of course, baking. Mixing thick muffin batter together and bringing overripe bananas back to life in bread are some of my favorite early morning rituals. And after all that, I'm usually hungry for a hearty blueberry muffin (page 14) or a thick slice of apple bread (page 2) myself!

The breads and muffins in this chapter have thick but delicate batters and should not be overmixed. The secret to fluffy muffins is to mix the dry and wet ingredients until just combined and no more. Overmixing will lead to a dense, tough texture. You'll notice that all of the muffin recipes are baked at two different temperatures: an initial high temperature for 5 minutes, then a lower temperature for the remainder of the bake time. This initial burst of very hot air will allow the muffin to rise up quickly, creating a beautiful dome.

Unglazed breads and muffins can be frozen for up to 3 months. My freezer is currently full of them! A quick 15 seconds in the microwave should do the trick before devouring.

BROWN SUGAR GLAZED APPLE BREAD

If you only make one apple bread in your lifetime, this is the recipe you need. One taste and you'll be sold, I promise! Quite a bold statement for apples, right? But this is the kind of soft, dense bread you'll want to have around for coffee, snack time, and unexpected guests. Sweet enough to fit the dessert category but humble enough for breakfast. The yogurt and eggs leave it fabulously moist, and the thick brown-sugar glaze smothers the bread and knocks it out of the park!

Prep time: 25 minutes • **Total time:** 1 hour, 30 minutes, plus cooling • **Makes:** 1 loaf

Apple Bread

¼ cup (60g) butter, softened to room temperature

¾ cup (180g) plain yogurt (Greek or regular)

⅓ cup (65g) dark brown sugar

⅔ cup (130g) granulated sugar

2 eggs

2 tsp vanilla extract

2 cups (250g) all-purpose flour

2 tsp baking powder

½ tsp baking soda

1½ tsp ground cinnamon

¾ tsp salt

1 large Granny Smith apple, peeled and diced

1 cup (140g) chopped pecans

Brown Sugar Glaze

1 cup (170g) dark brown sugar

¼ cup (60g) butter

⅓ cup (80ml) heavy cream

½ cup (60g) confectioners' sugar, sifted

1   Adjust the oven rack to the lower third position and preheat the oven to 350°F (175°C). Spray a 9 x 5-in (23 x 13 cm) loaf pan with non-stick spray and set aside.

2   **MAKE THE BREAD:** In a large bowl using a handheld mixer or stand mixer fitted with a paddle attachment, beat the butter, yogurt, brown sugar, and granulated sugar on medium speed until creamed, about 2–3 minutes. Add the eggs, one at a time, beating well after each addition. Scrape down the sides of the bowl as needed. Add the vanilla and beat on medium speed until everything is combined, about 2 full minutes. Remove the bowl from the mixer if using a stand mixer. Set aside.

3   In a medium bowl, whisk the flour, baking powder, baking soda, cinnamon, and salt together. Using a large spoon or rubber spatula, slowly mix the dry ingredients into the wet ingredients. Slowly stir everything together until no more flour pockets remain. The batter will be thick, but do not overmix it. Fold in the chopped apple and ⅔ cup (93g) of the pecans.

4   Spoon into the prepared loaf pan and bake for 55–65 minutes, making sure to loosely cover the loaf with aluminum foil halfway through cooking to prevent the top from getting too brown. The loaf is done when a toothpick inserted in the center comes out clean. Allow the loaf to cool completely in the pan on a wire rack.

5   **MAKE THE GLAZE:** Combine the brown sugar, butter, and heavy cream in a medium saucepan over a medium heat. Bring to a boil, stirring the mixture often. Allow to boil for 1 minute, then turn the heat down to low and allow to simmer for 1 minute. Remove from the heat and whisk in the confectioners' sugar. Add the remaining ⅓ cup (47g) of pecans. Allow to cool for 3 minutes then spoon over bread while it is still warm. The bread stays fresh in an airtight container at room temperature for up to 5 days and in the refrigerator for up to 7. Serve warm or cold.

 SALLY SAYS: I love using this brown-sugar glaze on top of muffins, cakes, and even pumpkin bread (page 9). Add a dash of salt, and you'll have a glaze that tastes just like salted caramel. The best part? This glaze can be made in advance, so once you're ready to use it, simply warm it on the stove for 3 minutes then spoon it over the bread.

GLAZED LEMON LOAF

I recently ate the best piece of lemon pound cake in the world from one of my favorite local coffee shops. It was rich, tender, and unbelievably moist—a perfect match for my iced coffee. I vowed to recreate it at home just for this cookbook and, of course, to save from splurging on pound cake at $4 per slice! The version I made isn't quite as heavy as pound cake, which is why I call it a loaf or quickbread. My loaf is bursting with one of my favorite baking flavors: lemon—and I mean lemon from freshly squeezed lemons, none of that lemon extract stuff! The batter comes together rather quickly and is made from ingredients you probably have in your pantry right now. So save yourself a trip to the coffee shop and make this sunshine-sweet loaf at home!

Prep time: 20 minutes • **Total time:** 1 hour, 10 minutes, plus cooling • **Makes:** 1 loaf

LEMON LOAF

1½ cups (190g) all-purpose flour

1 tsp baking powder

pinch salt

½ cup (115g) salted butter, softened to room temperature

1 cup (200g) granulated sugar

2 eggs

1½ tsp vanilla extract

juice of 1 large lemon (about 2 tbsp)

zest of 2 large lemons

½ cup (120ml) milk

GLAZE

juice of 1 large lemon

1 cup (120g) confectioners' sugar

1   Adjust the oven rack to the lower third position. Preheat the oven to 350°F (175°C). Generously spray a 9 x 5-in (23 x 13cm) loaf pan with non-stick spray. Set aside.

2   **MAKE THE LOAF:** Whisk the flour, baking powder, and salt together in a medium bowl. Set aside.

3   Using a hand-held mixer or stand mixer fitted with a paddle attachment, cream the softened butter in a medium bowl on medium speed for 1 minute. Once it is creamy and smooth, add the granulated sugar. Beat on medium speed until light in color. Beat in the eggs and vanilla until combined. Scrape down the sides of the bowl as needed. Add the lemon juice and zest and beat on medium speed for 1 minute. Slowly add the dry ingredients to the wet ingredients, alternating with the milk and beating well after each addition. Do not overmix.

4   Pour the batter into the prepared loaf pan and bake for 40–50 minutes, making sure to loosely cover the loaf with aluminum foil halfway through to prevent the top from getting too brown. The loaf is done when a toothpick inserted in the center comes out clean. Allow to cool completely in the pan on a wire rack.

5   **MAKE THE GLAZE:** Stir the lemon juice and confectioners' sugar together in a small bowl until smooth. Drizzle the glaze directly onto the loaf before cutting into slices. The loaf will stay fresh in an airtight container at room temperature for up to 2 days or in the refrigerator for up to 5.

 SALLY SAYS: This lemon glaze is so easy to prepare! If you'd like it thicker, add more confectioners' sugar, keeping in mind that this will make the glaze sweeter as well. Feel free to add a pinch of salt to cut the sweetness. Drizzle the glaze immediately before slicing and serving the loaf.

BUTTERSCOTCH STREUSEL BANANA BREAD

Traditional banana bread suddenly gets a flavor kick with the addition of a cinnamon-spiced butterscotch streusel. The combination of butterscotch and banana is perfection and works so well in this incredibly tender loaf, which is made moist with the addition of yogurt. You'll never want to make plain banana bread again; it's love at first bite!

Prep time: 20 minutes • **Total time:** 1 hour, 25 minutes, plus cooling • **Makes:** 1 loaf

Butterscotch Streusel

⅓ cup (40g) all-purpose flour

¼ cup (50g) dark brown sugar

½ tsp ground cinnamon

¼ cup (60g) butter, cold and cubed

⅓ cup (85g) plus 2 tbsp butterscotch chips

Banana Bread

½ cup (115g) unsalted butter, softened to room temperature

¾ cup (150g) dark brown sugar

2 eggs

⅓ cup (80g) Greek yogurt (or regular yogurt, plain or vanilla)

2 cups (450g) mashed bananas (about 4 large ripe bananas)

1 tsp vanilla extract

2 cups (250g) all-purpose flour

1 tsp baking soda

¼ tsp salt

½ tsp ground cinnamon

½ cup (70g) chopped pecans

1 Adjust the oven rack to the lower third position and preheat the oven to 350°F (175°C). Lightly spray a 9 x 5-in (23 x 13cm) loaf pan with non-stick spray. Set aside.

2 **MAKE THE STREUSEL:** Combine the flour, brown sugar, and cinnamon together in a medium-sized bowl. Cut the butter into the mixture with a pastry blender or mix with hands until it resembles coarse crumbs. Mix in ⅓ cup (85g) of butterscotch chips. Set aside.

3 **MAKE THE BREAD:** In a large bowl using a hand-held or stand mixer fitted with a paddle attachment, cream the butter and brown sugar together on medium speed, about 3 minutes. Add the eggs one at a time, beating well after each addition. Scrape down the sides of the bowl as needed. Add the yogurt, mashed bananas, and vanilla. Beat on medium speed for 2 minutes. Remove the bowl from the mixer if using a stand mixer. Set aside.

4 In a large bowl, whisk the flour, baking soda, salt, and cinnamon together. Using a large spoon or rubber spatula, slowly mix the dry ingredients into the wet ingredients until no more flour pockets remain. Do not overmix. Fold in the pecans.

5 Spoon the batter into the prepared baking pan. Top with the butterscotch streusel. Bake for 60–65 minutes, making sure to loosely cover the bread with aluminum foil halfway through cooking to prevent the top from getting too brown. The bread is done when a toothpick inserted in the center comes out clean.

6 Remove from the oven and sprinkle with the remaining 2 tablespoons of butterscotch chips. Allow the bread to cool completely in the pan on a wire rack before removing and slicing. The loaf will stay fresh in an airtight container at room temperature or in the refrigerator for up to 7 days.

 SALLY SAYS: This banana bread is my go-to recipe. Sometimes I skip the butterscotch streusel and top it with a tangy cream cheese frosting instead (page 144).

PUMPKIN CHOCOLATE CHIP BREAD

There are a million things I look forward to each October. Crisp air, crunchy leaves, Halloween, cardigans, and a whole lot of pumpkins. It's the time of year you can squeeze pumpkin into just about anything, including this bread. I call it my "disappearing quickbread" because whenever I make it, the slices are gobbled up within a day—and mostly by me! The flavorful spices and chocolate chips dancing inside this moist pumpkin bread are completely irresistible. Be sure to buy a few cans of pumpkin because when you try this bread, you'll want to make it again and again.

Prep time: 10 minutes • **Total time:** 1 hour, 15 minutes, plus cooling • **Makes:** 1 loaf

1¾ cups (220g) all-purpose flour

1 cup (200g) granulated sugar

½ cup (100g) light brown sugar

1 tsp baking soda

2 tsp ground cinnamon

¼ tsp ground nutmeg

¼ tsp ground cloves

¾ tsp salt

2 eggs

1½ cups (340g) pumpkin purée

½ cup (120ml) vegetable oil

¼ cup (60ml) orange juice

⅔ cup (120g) semi-sweet chocolate chips

1   Adjust the oven rack to the lower third position and preheat the oven to 350°F (175°C). Spray a 9 x 5-in (23 x 13cm) loaf pan with non-stick cooking spray. Set aside.

2   In a large bowl, whisk the flour, granulated sugar, brown sugar, baking soda, cinnamon, nutmeg, cloves, and salt together, making sure to break up any large brown sugar lumps. Set aside.

3   In a medium bowl, whisk the eggs. Add the pumpkin, vegetable oil, and orange juice, whisking until combined. Pour the wet ingredients into the flour mixture and gently mix together using a rubber spatula or wooden spoon. There will be a few lumps. Do not overmix the batter. Gently fold in the chocolate chips.

4   Pour into the prepared baking pan. Bake for 60–65 minutes, making sure to loosely cover the bread with aluminum foil halfway through to prevent the top from getting too brown. The bread is done when a toothpick inserted in the center comes out clean. Allow to cool in the pan on a wire rack before removing and cutting. The bread will stay fresh in an airtight container at room temperature or in the refrigerator for up to 10 days.

 SALLY SAYS: I like to taste the batter before pouring it into the loaf pan. Sometimes I stir in more ground cloves, sometimes more ground nutmeg. Go by your preference. Make sure you use pumpkin purée for this recipe though, not pumpkin pie filling. Canned or homemade purée will work just fine.

NUTELLA®-STUFFED CINNAMON-SUGAR MUFFINS

They may look like muffins, but a dunk in melted butter and a generous roll in cinnamon-sugar makes these baked breakfast treats taste like donuts, without the hassle of frying. Hiding inside each muffin is a sweet Nutella® surprise, which is layered into the batter as you fill the muffin pan. The muffins are ready in a jiffy, making them perfect for busy mornings. Sometimes I double the recipe and send them along with Kevin to work. His co-workers are always thankful!

Prep time: 20 minutes • **Total time:** 45 minutes • **Makes:** 8 muffins

MUFFINS

⅓ cup (75g) butter, softened to room temperature

½ cup (100g) granulated sugar

1 egg

1 tsp vanilla extract

½ cup (120ml) milk

1½ cups (190g) white whole wheat flour

1½ tsp baking powder

½ tsp ground cinnamon

¼ tsp ground nutmeg

½ tsp salt

8 tsp Nutella®

CINNAMON-SUGAR TOPPING

3 tbsp butter

¼ cup (50g) granulated sugar

2 tsp ground cinnamon

1 Preheat the oven to 425°F (220°C). Spray the muffin pan with non-stick cooking spray. Set aside.

2 Using a handheld or stand mixer fitted with a paddle attachment, beat the butter and granulated sugar together in a large bowl on medium speed until creamed, about 2 minutes. Beat in the egg, vanilla, and milk. Scrape down the sides of the bowl as needed. Using a large rubber spatula or wooden spoon, gently stir in the flour, baking powder, cinnamon, nutmeg, and salt until combined. Do not overmix.

3 Spoon 1 heaping tablespoon of batter into a muffin cup. Layer with 1 teaspoon of Nutella® in the center and spoon another heaping tablespoon of batter on top. If the muffin cups are completely full, that is ok. They will not overflow while baking. Repeat layering batter and Nutella® into each muffin tin for all 8 muffins. Fill the unused cups one-third full with water to prevent the pan from warping.

4 Bake at 425°F (220°C) for 5 minutes and then, leaving the muffins in the oven, reduce the temperature to 350°F (175°C) and bake for an additional 13–16 minutes, until the batter is set. Allow the muffins to cool in the pan for about 5 minutes.

5 **FOR THE TOPPING:** Melt the butter in a small bowl or pan. In a separate small bowl, mix the sugar and cinnamon together. Dip the top of each muffin into the melted butter and then dip into the cinnamon-sugar mixture. Swirl them around in the cinnamon-sugar a bit to make sure you get a thick coating. Set upright on a cooling rack. The muffins will stay fresh in an airtight container at room temperature for up to 3 days or in the refrigerator for up to 5.

 SALLY SAYS: I use white whole wheat flour in this recipe, which has the same nutrient value as whole wheat flour but tastes milder and lighter. If you can't find white whole wheat flour you can use all-purpose flour or a mix of whole wheat flour and all-purpose flour.

LEMON POPPY-SEED MUFFINS

When I began to brainstorm recipes for this cookbook, these muffins were one of the first to make the cut. I always like to make them when spring rolls around and we kiss those cold winter days goodbye. Their flavor is perfectly balanced between tart and sweet; there's plenty of zing but not so much that you pucker up your lips after each bite. The addition of Greek yogurt gives them a protein punch while leaving them extra-moist inside. No need to lug out your mixer either, these muffins come together by hand in minutes!

Prep time: 10 minutes • **Total time:** 30 minutes, plus cooling • **Makes:** 12 muffins

2½ cups (315g) all-purpose flour

½ cup (100g) granulated sugar

¼ cup (50g) light brown sugar

3 tbsp poppy seeds

2 tsp baking powder

¼ tsp baking soda

½ tsp salt

½ cup (115g) salted butter, melted

juice and zest of 3 medium lemons

2 eggs

½ cup (120g) non-fat or low-fat Greek yogurt (plain or vanilla flavored)

coarse sugar, for sprinkling

1   Preheat the oven to 425°F (220°C). Spray a 12-count muffin pan with non-stick spray. Set aside.

2   In a large bowl, whisk the flour, granulated sugar, brown sugar, poppy seeds, baking powder, baking soda, and salt together until thoroughly mixed. Set aside.

3   In a medium bowl, whisk the melted butter, lemon juice, and lemon zest together until combined. Add the eggs, one at a time, whisking after each addition. Whisk in the yogurt. Pour the wet ingredients into the dry ingredients and gently mix together until no pockets of flour remain. Do not overmix.

4   Spoon the thick batter into the muffin tins, filling each cup all the way to the top. Sprinkle each with coarse sugar. Bake for 5 minutes at 425°F (220°C) and then, keeping the muffins in the oven, reduce the oven temperature to 375°F (190°C) and continue to bake for 10–13 minutes longer, until the tops are lightly golden. A toothpick inserted in the center should come out clean. Allow to cool for 10 minutes. Muffins will stay fresh in an airtight container at room temperature for up to 5 days.

 SALLY SAYS: I like to add coarse sugar on top for two reasons. Not only does it sweeten the muffin tops ever so slightly, but the sugar also provides a nice crunchy texture in each bite. If you have trouble finding it in stores, coarse sugar is also known as decorating sugar or sugar crystals. I buy Wilton's® brand of "Sparkling Sugar" which is found next to the sprinkles in the baking aisle. You can also use Sugar in the Raw®.

JUMBO BLUEBERRY STREUSEL MUFFINS

I call this multi-purpose muffin batter my "master batter." It's a straightforward recipe to which you can add any of your favorite muffin extras. I personally love blueberries or juicy mangoes. The sky-high, soft, and tender muffins have that coveted bakery-style look to them. You can get that same finish by using a few of my secrets—baking at a high initial temperature, using enough leavener, and generously topping them with streusel, of course.

Prep time: 20 minutes • **Total time:** 50 minutes, plus cooling • **Makes:** 6 in a jumbo muffin pan*

Streusel Topping

½ cup (100g) granulated sugar

⅓ cup (40g) all-purpose flour

1 tsp ground cinnamon

¼ cup (60g) butter, cold

Muffins

3 cups (375g) all-purpose flour

4 tsp baking powder

1 tsp salt

1 tsp ground cinnamon

2 eggs, at room temperature (see *Sally Says,* right)

¾ cup (150g) granulated sugar

¼ cup (50g) light brown sugar

1 cup (240ml) milk, at room temperature

½ cup (120ml) vegetable oil

1 tsp vanilla extract

1¼ cup (215g) fresh or frozen blueberries (do not thaw)

1. Preheat the oven to 425°F (220°C). Spray a 6-count jumbo muffin pan* with non-stick spray or line the cups with muffin liners. Set aside.

2. **MAKE THE STREUSEL TOPPING:** Combine the granulated sugar, flour, and cinnamon in a small bowl. Cut in the cold butter and mix around with a pastry blender or your hands until coarse crumbs form. Set aside.

3. **MAKE THE MUFFINS:** In a large bowl, gently toss together the flour, baking powder, salt, and cinnamon. Set aside.

4. In a medium bowl, whisk the eggs, granulated sugar, and brown sugar together until combined. Mix in milk, oil, and vanilla. The mixture will be pale and yellow. Fold the wet ingredients into the dry ingredients and mix everything together gently by hand. Avoid over-mixing, though no big pockets of flour should be remaining. The batter will be extremely thick and somewhat lumpy. Fold in the blueberries.

5. Pour the batter into prepared muffin tins, filling all the way to the top. Top each with streusel. Bake at 425°F (220°C) for 5 minutes and then, keeping the muffins in the oven, reduce the temperature to 375°F (190°) and continue to bake for 25–26 minutes, until the tops are lightly golden. A toothpick inserted in the center should come out clean. Allow to cool for 10 minutes. The muffins taste best eaten the same day, though you can store them at room temperature in an airtight container for up to 5 days.

 SALLY SAYS: It's important to use room-temperature eggs in recipes that call for it because they disperse more evenly into a batter, creating a lighter and fluffier texture. In a hurry? You can bring eggs to room temperature in a jiffy! Simply place the eggs in a glass of warm water and let sit for 5–10 minutes as you get your other ingredients ready.

* For 16 standard-size muffins, reduce the baking time to 17–18 minutes with the first 5 minutes at the 425°F (220°C) temperature and the remaining 12–13 minutes at 375°C (190°C).

MIGHTY MANGO MUFFINS

A friend once asked me, "If you could eat one food for the rest of your life, what would it be?" My answer wasn't pizza or chocolate cake or even ice cream … it was mangoes! When I began to write this cookbook, I knew I had to incorporate my favorite food into a new recipe, so I chose to make cinnamon-spiced muffins. Each buttery bite is moist and exploding with juicy mangoes!

Prep time: 15 minutes • **Total time:** 35 minutes, plus cooling • **Makes:** 12 muffins

MUFFINS

1¾ cup (220g) all-purpose flour

2½ teaspoons baking powder

½ teaspoon salt

½ teaspoon ground cinnamon

⅓ cup (75g) unsalted butter, melted

⅔ cup (134g) light brown sugar

1 large egg

¾ cup (180ml) milk

1⅓ cup (150g) chopped fresh or frozen mangoes (do not thaw)

TOPPING

2 tbsp granulated sugar

½ teaspoon ground cinnamon

1 Preheat oven to 425°F (220°C). Spray a 12-count muffin pan with non-stick spray. Set aside.

2 **MAKE THE MUFFINS:** In a large bowl, gently toss the flour, baking powder, salt, and cinnamon together. Set aside.

3 In a medium bowl, whisk the melted butter and brown sugar together until combined. Mixture will be thick and gritty. Whisk in the egg, then the milk. Fold wet ingredients into dry ingredients and mix everything together gently by hand. Avoid over-mixing. The batter will be extremely thick and somewhat lumpy. Fold in the mangoes.

4 **MAKE THE TOPPING:** Combine the granulated sugar and cinnamon together in a small bowl. Spoon the batter into prepared muffin cups, filling all the way to the top. Sprinkle cinnamon-sugar over each. Bake at 425°F (220°C) for 5 minutes. Keeping the muffins in the oven, reduce oven temperature to 375°F (190°C), and continue to bake for 12–13 minutes, until tops are lightly golden. A toothpick inserted in the center should come out clean. Allow to cool for 10 minutes. Muffins taste best if you serve fresh on the same day, but you can store them at room temperature in an airtight container for up to 5 days.

 SALLY SAYS: Fresh mangoes freeze well. When I find them on sale during their peak summer season, I dice them up and freeze them in zipped-top bags. That way I always have some on hand for making these fruity muffins.

DOUBLE CHOCOLATE MUFFINS

My treat for going to the grocery store with my mom when I was little was a giant chocolate muffin from the store's bakery. It was the size of my head and quite the decadent breakfast! The fond memories I have of that delectable treat meant that I had to include a classic chocolate muffin recipe in this cookbook—a muffin like that same, moist, fudgy one I grew up loving. The batter comes together quickly, making these the perfect treat to whip up any morning of the week. Besides, who doesn't love waking up to chocolate (or double chocolate!) for breakfast?

Prep time: 10 minutes • **Total time:** 30 minutes • **Makes:** 12 muffins

2 cups (250g) all-purpose flour

1 cup (200g) granulated sugar

½ tsp salt

½ cup (64g) unsweetened cocoa powder

1 tsp baking soda

1 cup (180g) semi-sweet chocolate chips

2 eggs

¾ cup (185g) plain yogurt (Greek or regular)

½ cup (120ml) vegetable oil

½ cup (120ml) milk

1   Preheat the oven to 425°F (220°C). Spray one 12-count muffin pan with non-stick spray. Set aside.

2   In a large bowl, whisk the flour, granulated sugar, salt, cocoa powder, and baking soda together until thoroughly combined. Mix in the chocolate chips. Set aside.

3   In a medium bowl, whisk the eggs, yogurt, oil, and milk until combined. Fold the wet ingredients into the dry ingredients and gently mix together until no pockets of flour remain. Do not overmix.

4   Spoon the thick batter into the muffin pan, filling each cup all the way to the top. Bake for 5 minutes at 425°F (220°C) and then, keeping the muffins in the oven, reduce the oven temperature to 350°F (175°C), and continue to bake for 12–14 minutes. A toothpick inserted in the center should come out clean. Allow to cool for 10 minutes. Muffins taste best served fresh on the same day, but you can store them at room temperature in an airtight container for up to 5 days.

BREAKFAST

They say breakfast is the most important meal of the day. I say it's the only excuse to eat sweets and call it a meal! The following recipes, ranging from pastries and pancakes to donuts and crumb cakes, are decadent wake-up calls for your taste buds. They're the kind of delightful dishes you slow down for on lazy Sundays with a steaming cup of coffee.

Most of the recipes in this chapter are easy to prepare, some even taking less than 40 minutes to make from start to finish. If you're entertaining, recipes such as Overnight French Toast Bake (page 32) and Strawberry Rolls with Vanilla Glaze (page 23) are easy to prep the night before and will dazzle your guests in the morning. Have your little ones lend a hand with Baked Powdered Sugar Donuts (page 27) and Peanut Butter and Jelly Turnovers (page 31), both simple recipes created with kids in mind.

So whether you're planning a morning meal for your family or a fancy brunch for guests, I know you'll find that perfect recipe to please everyone at the table. Go ahead and indulge!

STRAWBERRY ROLLS WITH VANILLA GLAZE

There is nothing quite like sinking your teeth into a fluffy sweet roll first thing in the morning—especially if that roll is tender, soft, and loaded with a succulent strawberry filling. This yeasted dough recipe is different from most; it only requires one rise, which considerably reduces the total preparation time. It's a great recipe for yeast beginners. I love topping the gooey strawberry rolls with a shower of vanilla glaze, because in my world, no sweet roll is complete without it!

Prep time: 30 minutes • **Total time:** 2 hours, 25 minutes • **Makes:** 10–11 rolls

FILLING

1½ cups (190g) finely chopped strawberries

⅓ cup (70g) granulated sugar

1½ tbsp cornstarch

DOUGH

2¾ cups (345g) all-purpose flour, plus extra for dusting

3 tbsp granulated sugar

1 tsp salt

2¼ tsp instant dry yeast (1 standard packet)

½ cup (120ml) water

¼ cup (60ml) milk

2½ tbsp butter

1 egg

GLAZE

1 cup (120g) confectioners' sugar

1 tsp vanilla extract

2 tbsp heavy cream or milk

1 **MAKE THE FILLING:** Warm the diced strawberries in a small saucepan over a medium heat. Stir constantly for 4 minutes until the strawberry juices have been released. Add the granulated sugar and cornstarch and continue to stir for another 2 minutes. The mixture will thicken. Remove from the heat and chill until ready to use. The filling must be very cold.

2 **MAKE THE DOUGH:** In a large bowl, toss 2¼ cups (280g) flour, the granulated sugar, salt, and yeast together until evenly dispersed. Set aside.

3 Heat the water, milk, and butter together in the microwave until the butter is melted and the mixture is hot to touch—about 110–115°F (45–50°C). Stir the butter mixture into the flour mixture. Add the egg and add at least ⅓ cup (40g) of additional flour to make a soft dough. You may need up to ½ cup (63g) if your dough is too wet. The dough will be ready when it gently pulls away from the side of the bowl and has an elastic consistency.

4 On a lightly floured work surface, knead the dough for 3 minutes. Lightly spray a bowl with non-stick spray and set the dough inside. Let rest for 10 minutes.

5 After 10 minutes, roll the dough out into a 14 x 8-in (35 x 20cm) rectangle. Spread the strawberry filling on top. Roll up the dough tightly along the long edge. Cut into 10–11 even pieces and arrange them in a lightly greased 9-in (23cm) round or square pan. Loosely cover the rolls with aluminum foil and allow to rise in a warm, draft-free place for 1–1½ hours. (See *Sally Says,* opposite page)

6 After the rolls have doubled in size, preheat the oven to 375°F (190°C). Bake for 25–30 minutes, until lightly browned. After 15 minutes, rotate the pan in the oven and loosely cover the rolls with aluminum foil to avoid heavy browning.

7 **MAKE THE GLAZE:** Mix the confectioners' sugar, vanilla, and cream together until smooth and drizzle over the rolls immediately before serving. These rolls taste best served on the same day. Unglazed rolls may be frozen for up to 2 months.

GRANDMA'S STICKY PECAN ROLLS

It's not the holidays without a pan of these sticky rolls. Growing up, my grandma baked a batch on Thanksgiving morning and my mom made them again every Christmas brunch. Over the years, I've updated the dough recipe slightly, and now it's the same easy yeast dough I use in Strawberry Rolls (page 23), but they're still every bit as sticky, sweet, and as fluffy as I can remember. When I was little, I always peeled off the gooey pecans and put them on my mom's plate. Now the pecans are my favorite part!

Prep time: 30 minutes • **Total time:** 2 hours, 25 minutes • **Makes:** 10 rolls

PECAN TOPPING

¾ cup (100g) chopped pecans

6 tbsp butter, melted

½ cup (100g) dark brown sugar

2 tbsp light corn syrup

DOUGH

2¾ cups (345g) all-purpose flour, plus more for kneading

3 tbsp granulated sugar

1 tsp salt

2¼ tsp instant dry yeast (1 standard packet)

½ cup (120ml) water

¼ cup (60ml) milk

2½ tbsp butter

1 egg

FILLING

½ cup (100g) granulated sugar

2 tsp ground cinnamon

1 **MAKE THE PECAN TOPPING:** Evenly layer the pecans in a lightly greased 9-in round or square pan. In a small bowl, whisk the melted butter, dark brown sugar, and corn syrup together until smooth. Pour over the pecans. Set aside.

2 **MAKE THE DOUGH:** In a large bowl, toss 2¼ (280g) cups flour, granulated sugar, salt, and yeast together until evenly dispersed. Set aside.

3 Heat the water, milk, and butter together in the microwave until the butter is melted and the mixture is hot to the touch—about 110°F–115°F (45-50°C). Stir the butter mixture into the flour mixture. Add the egg and at least ⅓ cup (40g) of additional flour to make a soft dough. You may need up to ½ cup (63g) if your dough is too wet. The dough will be ready when it gently pulls away from the side of the bowl and has an elastic consistency.

4 On a lightly floured work surface, knead the dough for 3 minutes. Lightly spray a bowl with non-stick spray and set the dough inside. Let rest for 10 minutes.

5 **FILL THE ROLLS:** After 10 minutes, roll the dough out into a 14 x 8-in (35 x 20cm) rectangle. Combine the granulated sugar and cinnamon and sprinkle on top of the dough. Roll up the dough tightly along the long edge. Cut into 10 even pieces (each roughly 1½ in (4cm) wide) and arrange on top of the pecans. Loosely cover the rolls with aluminum foil and allow to rise in a warm, draft-free place for 1–1½ hours.

6 After the rolls have doubled in size, preheat the oven to 375°F (190°C). Bake for 25–30 minutes, until lightly browned. After 15 minutes, rotate the pan in the oven and loosely cover the rolls with aluminum foil to avoid heavy browning.

7 Remove from the oven and allow to slightly cool for at least 10 minutes before serving. You can either invert the pan onto a large plate or cut the rolls directly out of the pan. These rolls taste best enjoyed on the same day, or they may be frozen for up to 2 months.

BAKED POWDERED SUGAR DONUTS

Making donuts at home is shockingly simple. In fact, I bet making a batch of these is quicker than trekking to your local doughnut shop. I love these baked donuts because there's no extra grease taking away from their classic cakey texture. Do yourself a favor and buy a donut pan. They are very inexpensive and after one taste of these sugary breakfast treats, you'll be thankful you have one around!

Prep time: 15 minutes • **Total time:** 25 minutes • **Makes:** 8 donuts

1 cup (125g) all-purpose flour

1 tsp baking powder

¼ tsp baking soda

½ tsp ground cinnamon

pinch ground nutmeg

⅓ cup (65g) granulated sugar

¼ cup (60ml) milk

¼ cup (60g) Greek yogurt
(or regular yogurt, plain or vanilla)

1 egg

2 tbsp butter, melted

2 tsp vanilla extract

1 cup (120g) confectioner's sugar,
plus more if needed

1 Preheat the oven to 350°F (175°C). Spray a donut pan with non-stick spray. Set aside.

2 Whisk the flour, baking powder, baking soda, cinnamon, nutmeg, and granulated sugar together in a medium bowl. Set aside.

3 Whisk the milk, yogurt, and egg together until smooth. Add the melted butter and vanilla, whisking until fully combined. Pour the wet ingredients into the dry ingredients and stir until just combined. Do not overmix. The batter will be very thick.

4 Spoon the batter into the donut cups—I highly recommend using a large zipped-top bag for ease. Cut a corner off the bottom of the bag and pipe the batter into each donut cup, filling ⅔–¾ of the way full. Bake for 9–10 minutes, or until the edges are lightly browned.

5 Pour the confectioner's sugar into a separate, large, zipped-top bag. Place the warm donuts inside and shake until they are fully coated in the sugar. Add more sugar if you'd like a thicker coating. Sugar the donuts immediately before serving. Donuts taste best eaten the same day, though they may be stored, covered, at room temperature for 2 days.

 SALLY SAYS: Pay attention to how high you're filling the donut cups with batter. Stick to ⅔–¾ of the way full. Any more than that and the donuts will puff up and you will lose the hole in the center. I often double this recipe for a larger group.

VANILLA CREPES WITH NUTELLA®

Homemade crepes are surprisingly easy and very inexpensive to prepare, and unquestionably delicious. Whenever we're in the mood for this French-style pancake, this is the recipe I use. They are the perfect lazy weekend breakfast with a steaming hot cup of coffee. Be sure to use a small frying pan, the exact size you'd like your crepes to be. Bon appétit!

Prep time: 30 minutes • **Total time:** 30 minutes • **Makes:** 8 crepes

1 cup (125g) all-purpose flour

1 tbsp granulated sugar

pinch salt

¾ cup (180ml) milk

½ cup (120ml) water

2 eggs

3 tbsp butter, melted and cooled to room temperature, plus extra for greasing

1 tbsp vanilla extract

½ cup (296g) Nutella® (or more)

confectioners' sugar, for dusting

1. Combine the flour, granulated sugar, salt, milk, water, eggs, melted butter, and vanilla in a blender. Mix on medium speed for 20 seconds, or until everything is combined. The mixture will be very thick and creamy. Pour the mixture into a medium-size bowl and set aside.

2. Melt a little butter in a small frying pan over a medium heat. Pour ¼ cup (50g) of batter onto the center of the pan. Tilt the pan and swirl the batter evenly to all sides. Cook for 1–2 minutes, or until the bottom is lightly browned. With a thin spatula, gently flip the crepe and cook for 1 more minute on the other side. Transfer the cooked crepe to a large plate and repeat with the remaining batter, making sure to butter the pan between each crepe, and to separate the cooked crepes with parchment paper.

3. Spread 1–2 tablespoons of Nutella® onto each crepe. Roll or fold into quarters and sprinkle with confectioners' sugar. Unfilled crepes will remain fresh in an airtight container in the refrigerator for 1 day or in the freezer for 2 months.

 SALLY SAYS: Get creative! This crepe recipe is endlessly adaptable with whatever fillings you like. Sometimes we use raspberry jam, lemon curd, fresh peaches, or even peanut butter.

PEANUT BUTTER AND JELLY TURNOVERS

I am a complete sucker for buttery, flaky puff pastry. I find its endless pillowy layers completely irresistible. I love filling it with homemade jam and making turnovers for breakfast. While I usually drizzle the golden-brown tops with vanilla glaze, I opted for a simple melted peanut butter drizzle one morning and have never gone back. If you think this recipe looks challenging, think again. You'll be enjoying a warm pastry reminiscent of your favorite childhood sandwich in under 45 minutes.

Prep time: 25 minutes • **Total time:** 45 minutes • **Makes:** 8 turnovers

3 tbsp cornstarch

2 tbsp warm water

3 cups (approx. 420g) mixed berries (frozen or fresh)

½ cup (100g) granulated sugar

1 tsp vanilla extract

1 package (2 sheets) frozen puff pastry, thawed

all-purpose flour, for dusting

1 egg, beaten

¼ cup (60g) creamy peanut butter, melted

1. Mix the cornstarch and warm water together in a small bowl until fully dissolved. In a medium saucepan over a medium heat, cook the cornstarch mixture, berries, granulated sugar, and vanilla together until the berries begin to break down. Stir constantly. After 5 minutes, stop stirring and allow to boil for 1 minute. Remove from the heat and allow the mixture to thicken for 15 minutes.

2. Adjust the oven rack to the lower third position and preheat the oven to 400°F (205°C). Line two large cookie sheets with parchment paper or silicone baking mats.

3. Unroll the puff pastry sheets onto a lightly floured surface. Cut each into 4 squares. Place 4 squares onto each prepared baking sheet and spoon 2–3 tablespoons of berry mixture onto the center of each square. Fold the pastry over to make a triangular package and crimp the edges with a fork to seal. Some berry juice may leak out.

4. Lightly brush the top of each turnover with beaten egg. Cut 2 or 3 small steam vents in the tops then bake each batch for 20 minutes, until golden brown. Rotate the pan halfway through bake time to avoid uneven browning.

5. Remove from the oven and drizzle each turnover with melted peanut butter immediately before serving. These turnovers taste best eaten on the same day, though you can store them at room temperature in an airtight container for up to 3 days.

 SALLY SAYS: Instead of peanut butter, try glazing the top of each turnover with vanilla glaze (page 23) or a simple dusting of confectioners' sugar.

OVERNIGHT FRENCH TOAST BAKE

This warm and cozy breakfast dish gets all the compliments without all the work. Instead of standing over the stove dipping and cooking each individual slice, just throw your French toast ingredients into a pan. For maximum flavor and moisture, I like to use a crusty loaf of French bread or braided challah. Thick, hearty slices of either will soak up all of the brown sugar and cinnamon flavors as it chills overnight. The only thing left to do in the morning is to bake and indulge!

Prep time: 15 minutes • **Total time:** 1 hour, plus overnight chilling • **Serves:** 6–8

3 tbsp light corn syrup

1½ cups (200g) dark brown sugar

¾ cup (170g) butter

1 x 12–14oz (340–400g) loaf French bread or challah (day-old or stale is preferred)

5 eggs, beaten

1 tbsp vanilla extract

1½ cups (360ml) milk

1 tsp ground cinnamon

confectioners' sugar for sprinkling (optional)

1 Heat the corn syrup, brown sugar, and butter together in a small saucepan over a medium heat. Remove from the heat once the butter is melted and spread into a 9 x 13-in (23–33cm) baking pan.

2 Slice the bread into 10–12 thick slices. Layer on top of the brown sugar mixture. Set aside.

3 Whisk the beaten eggs, vanilla, milk, and cinnamon together in a large bowl. Pour over the bread. Cover the pan tightly and chill for 8 hours or overnight in the refrigerator.

4 Preheat the oven to 350°F (175°C). Bake, covered with aluminum foil, for 45 minutes, or until the bread is cooked through. Sprinkle with confectioners' sugar prior to serving. This bake tastes best served on the same day.

 SALLY SAYS: Let your imagination run wild with different variations! When I make this dish around the holidays, I like adding two thinly sliced apples and ½ cup (60g) of dried cranberries to the bottom of the pan with the syrup mixture. For a fall treat, I replace 1 egg with 1 scant cup (228g) of pumpkin purée—pour this on top of the bread and sprinkle with chopped pecans and pumpkin pie spice.

BLUEBERRY BUTTERMILK PANCAKES

A tall stack of pancakes with cascades of maple syrup and a pat of butter is the epitome of comfort food. Pancakes were always our standard weekend breakfast growing up. My sisters begged for chocolate chip, but I (shockingly) always wanted plain. Today, I'm all about the blueberries in this classic breakfast food. Two essentials for my pancakes? Real buttermilk and a hot skillet.

Prep time: 30 minutes • **Total time:** 30 minutes • **Makes:** 10–12 pancakes

6 tbsp butter, plus more
for greasing

2 cups (250g) all-purpose flour

¼ cup (50g) granulated sugar

1 tsp baking powder

½ tsp baking soda

¼ tsp salt

2 eggs

2 cups (480ml) buttermilk

1 cup blueberries
(fresh or frozen)

1 Melt the butter in a small bowl and allow to slightly cool.

2 Whisk the flour, granulated sugar, baking powder, baking soda, and salt together in a medium bowl. Set aside.

3 Whisk the eggs until beaten, then whisk in the buttermilk and melted butter. Whisk in the dry ingredients until just combined—a few small lumps are okay. The batter will be thick.

4 Melt a little butter in a large frying pan or a griddle over medium heat. Spoon ⅓ cup (45g) of batter onto the pan and repeat with 2–3 more pancakes depending on the size of your pan. Dot several blueberries on the top of each pancake—the amount of blueberries for each is up to you. Cook the pancakes until bubbles rise to the surface, about 2 minutes. Carefully flip the pancakes and cook for another 2 minutes. Butter the pan before each batch of remaining pancakes.

5 Transfer the pancakes to a large plate and cover tightly to keep warm as you prepare the remaining pancakes.

 SALLY SAYS: You can always add the blueberries straight to the batter before cooking. I prefer dotting each pancake with a bunch of them as it cooks because I can make sure each pancake has enough. Instead of blueberries, add chocolate chips, banana slices, or even sprinkle with cinnamon. If you're a purist like little Sally, feel free to leave the pancakes plain.

GLAZED CHERRY CRUMB CAKE

If you're anything like me, you love crumb cake mostly for the crumbs. The more crumbs, the better—and this breakfast cake is piled high with them! A touch of almond extract pairs wonderfully with the juicy cherries layered inside. And the drizzle of vanilla glaze puts this cake over the top! Trust me, your morning guests will be begging for a second slice.

Prep time: 20 minutes • **Total time:** 1 hour, 25 minutes • **Makes:** 10–12 servings

CRUMB TOPPING

¾ cup (95g) all-purpose flour

⅓ cup (67g) light brown sugar

¼ cup (50g) granulated sugar

1 tsp ground cinnamon

6 tbsp butter, cold and cubed

CAKE

1 egg

¼ cup (60g) butter, melted and cooled

½ cup (120ml) milk

2 tsp vanilla extract

1 tsp almond extract

1½ cups (190g) all-purpose flour

¾ cup (150g) granulated sugar

2 tsp baking powder

½ tsp salt

1 cup (225g) dark sweet cherries, pitted and chopped (see *Sally Says*, right)

1 tbsp cherry, raspberry, or strawberry preserves/jam

¼ cup (25g) slivered almonds

GLAZE

¾ cup (90g) confectioners' sugar, sifted

3 tsp milk

½ tsp vanilla extract

1   Adjust the oven rack to the lower third position. Preheat the oven to 350°F (175°C). Spray an 8-in (20cm) springform pan with non-stick spray. Set aside.

2   **MAKE THE CRUMB TOPPING:** Combine the flour, brown sugar, granulated sugar, and cinnamon together in a medium bowl. Cut the butter into the mixture with a pastry blender or mix with hands until it resembles coarse crumbs. Set aside.

3   **MAKE THE CAKE:** In a large bowl using a hand-held or stand mixer fitted with a paddle attachment, beat the egg and melted butter together on medium speed until combined. Do not do this by hand, you must use a mixer. Add the milk, vanilla, and almond extract and beat on medium speed until thoroughly mixed. Scrape down the sides of the bowl as needed. Set aside.

4   Whisk the flour, sugar, baking powder, and salt together in a medium bowl until combined. With the mixer running on low, pour the dry ingredients into the wet ingredients. Mix until just combined. Pour into the prepared baking pan.

5   Mix the chopped cherries and the jam together and spoon evenly over the batter. Top with the crumb topping, then the almonds. Gently press the topping into the batter.

6   Bake for 40–50 minutes, or until a toothpick inserted in the center of the cake comes out free of cake crumbs. Allow to cool in the pan on a wire rack for at least 20 minutes before glazing.

7   **MAKE THE GLAZE:** Stir the confectioners' sugar, milk, and vanilla together. Remove the sides of the springform pan and drizzle the glaze over the cake. The cake will stay fresh, covered, at room temperature for 4 days.

 SALLY SAYS: I use dark sweet cherries, whose peak is in the summertime. Chopped, frozen, dark cherries make a fine substitute. I like to mix the cherries with a bit of jam to make them extra juicy. If using chopped frozen cherries, skip the jam.

BROWNIES & BARS

Brownies and bars are easy to make. There are no individual cookies to roll, no dough to rise, no cake layers to cool, which means less hands-on work, less dishes, and more eating! Readers of my blog tell me they love these no-fuss desserts, so I've included extra recipes in this chapter for people who don't have all day to spend in the kitchen.

While they may be the simplest of recipes to follow, brownies and bars can also be over the top and decorative, finished with caramel swirls or minty frosting. They can also be as humble as a homemade fudge brownie or simple lemon bar. One thing is certain, though, the following recipes raise the bar for any ordinary brownie, cheesecake bar, or blondie you've ever tasted.

An important thing to note is that my brownies and bars are all made in baking pans, and I prefer aluminum foil over parchment paper for lining the pans because it molds more easily to the base. When lining, make sure there is enough overhang on the sides so that you can lift the bars out as a whole before slicing. Also be sure to evenly spread the batter in the pan. If one corner is thicker than the other, the bars will bake unevenly and could burn. Before cutting, be certain that the brownies and bars are no longer warm. These are just a few of the rookie errors I made when I first started out, and I wish someone had shared them with me back then. Happy baking!

FUDGE RIPPLE MONSTER BARS

Traditional monster cookies are oatmeal cookies with peanut butter, chocolate chips, and M&Ms®. Take those same ingredients, remix them, and you've got the monster cookie's funky younger sister. What you see here are soft peanut butter cookie bars, with lots of M&Ms®, and some chewy oats for texture. Instead of simply adding chocolate chips to the dough, I opted to melt them down into a fudge-like consistency to create a decadent ripple in the center. Try to resist sneaking a lick of the fudge ripple … I dare you!

Prep time: 20 minutes • **Total time:** 45 minutes, plus cooling • **Makes:** 16 bars

Monster Bars

1⅓ cups (170g) all-purpose flour

⅔ cup (60g) old-fashioned rolled oats

½ tsp baking soda

½ cup (115g) salted butter, softened to room temperature

½ cup (100g) light brown sugar

¼ cup (50g) granulated sugar

¾ cup (185g) creamy peanut butter

1 egg

1 tsp vanilla extract

¾ cup (150g) M&Ms®

Fudge Ripple Filling

7oz (200g or ½ x 14-oz can) sweetened condensed milk

1 tbsp salted butter

1 cup (180g) semi-sweet chocolate chips

1 tsp vanilla extract

1 Preheat the oven to 350°F (175°C). Line the bottom and sides of an 8 x 8-in (20 x 20cm) baking pan with aluminum foil, leaving an overhang on all sides. Set aside.

2 **MAKE THE BARS:** Whisk the flour, oats, and baking soda together in a large bowl. Set aside.

3 Using a handheld or stand mixer fitted with a paddle attachment, beat the butter, brown sugar, and granulated sugar together in a large bowl on medium speed until creamed, about 2–3 minutes. Add the peanut butter, egg, and vanilla one after the other, mixing after each addition. Scrape down the sides of the bowl as needed. With the mixer running on low, slowly add the dry ingredients into the wet ingredients until combined. Do not overmix.

4 Press two-thirds of the dough evenly into the prepared baking pan. Stir the M&Ms® into the remaining dough. Set aside while you make the fudge ripple filling.

5 **MAKE THE FUDGE RIPPLE:** In a small saucepan over a low heat, combine the sweetened condensed milk, butter, and chocolate chips. Stir until the chocolate chips are melted and the mixture is smooth. Remove from the heat and stir in the vanilla. Pour the fudge over the bottom layer of dough.

6 Mold the remaining dough containing M&Ms® into flat pieces and layer on top of the fudge filling. You won't have enough dough to make one single layer, so some of the filling will be exposed.

7 Bake for 25 minutes, or until the top is lightly browned. Allow to cool completely. Lift the foil out of the pan using the overhang on the sides and cut into bars. Bars stay fresh in an airtight container at room temperature or in the refrigerator for up to 1 week.

DEATH BY CHOCOLATE BROWNIES

Ditch that boxed brownie mix now! There is nothing in this world that compares to a homemade brownie, made 100 percent from scratch—especially a brownie recipe made in only one bowl! These easy chocolate-chunk brownies are moist, dense, and so rich that you'll swear you're eating fudge. Sometimes you need a chocolate fix, and these brownies are just what the doctor ordered.

Prep time: 20 minutes • **Total time:** 1–1 hour, 5 minutes, plus cooling • **Makes:** 20 brownies

½ cup (115g) salted butter

8oz (226g) coarsely chopped semi-sweet chocolate, such as Baker's brand

1 cup (200g) granulated sugar

3 eggs, cold

1 tsp vanilla extract

¾ cup (95g) all-purpose flour

¼ tsp salt

1½ cups (225g) semi-sweet chocolate chunks or chocolate chips

1   Melt the butter and chopped chocolate in a medium saucepan on a medium heat, stirring constantly, about 5 minutes. Remove from the heat, pour into a large bowl, and allow to slightly cool for 10 minutes.

2   Adjust the oven rack to the lower third position and preheat the oven to 350°F (175°C). Line the bottom and sides of an 11 x 7-in (28 x 18cm) baking pan with aluminum foil, leaving an overhang on all sides. Set aside.

3   Stir the granulated sugar into the cooled chocolate/butter mixture. Add in the eggs, one at a time, whisking until smooth after each addition. Whisk in the vanilla. Gently fold in the flour and salt, then the chocolate chunks until combined. Pour batter into the prepared pan and bake for 37–45 minutes, or until the brownies begin to pull away from the edges of the pan. A toothpick inserted in the center should come out with only a few moist crumbs when they are done.

4   Allow the brownies to cool completely in the pan set on a wire rack. Lift the foil out of the pan using the overhang on the sides and cut into squares. The brownies will stay fresh in an airtight container at room temperature for 1 week.

 SALLY SAYS: Did you know that a brownie's fudgy texture directly correlates with the amount of flour used in the recipe? I prefer chewy, fudgy brownies to cakey brownies, so this recipe uses as little flour as possible to provide that ultra-dense texture. If cakey brownies are your preference, use 1 full cup (125g) of all-purpose flour instead of ¾ cup (95g).

MINT CHOCOLATE FUDGE BROWNIES

Let me introduce you to the ultimate mint-chocolate creation. If you're looking for a decadent, rich, and blow-your-diet dessert, meet your new brownie friend. Take my favorite fudgy brownie recipe and dress it up by adding creamy, cool mint frosting and a sprinkle of chocolate chips. Warning: these fudgy brownies are not for the faint of heart, but they're worth every minute on the treadmill!

Prep time: 30 minutes • **Total time:** 1 hour, 15 minutes, plus cooling • **Makes:** 20 brownies

BROWNIES

1 batch Death by Chocolate Brownies (page 43)

MINT FROSTING

3 tbsp butter, softened to room temperature

2oz (50g) cream cheese, softened to room temperature

2 cups (240g) confectioners' sugar

3 tbsp heavy cream

¼ tsp peppermint extract (see *Sally Says*, right)

2 drops green liquid food coloring

⅓ cup (60g) mini chocolate chips

1 Make the Death by Chocolate Brownies following the recipe on page 43. When they are finished baking, allow them to cool completely in the pan on a wire rack. Lift the foil out of the pan using the overhang on the sides. Do not slice yet, just set the brownies aside.

2 **MAKE THE FROSTING:** Using a handheld or stand mixer fitted with a paddle attachment, beat the butter and cream cheese together in a medium bowl on medium speed for 1 minute. Add the confectioners' sugar and heavy cream. Switch to low speed and beat for 2–3 minutes, until smooth. Add the peppermint extract and food coloring and beat for 1 minute. Spread the frosting over the cooled brownies. Sprinkle with mini chocolate chips. Cut into squares, running the knife under hot water and patting dry between each cut. The brownies will stay fresh in an airtight container in the refrigerator for 5 days.

 SALLY SAYS: I like to slather this easy mint frosting recipe on chocolate cupcakes (page 151) or even sugar cookies (page 118) too. Use the peppermint extract sparingly; that stuff is strong. Begin with ¼ teaspoon, taste, and then add a bit more until the frosting is minty enough.

WHITE CHOCOLATE MACADAMIA NUT BLONDIES

Blondies are the seemingly virtuous little sister of the fudgy brownie (page 43). While they may look innocent, the kind of blondies I make can hold their own against their devilish chocolate counterparts. They're delightfully buttery, allowing the tastes of white chocolate and macadamias to shine through. I sweeten the blondies almost exclusively with brown sugar to give them a soft, moist interior and a subtle molasses flavor. I'm a sucker for these dense little blondies, and I promise it has nothing to do with my hair color!

Prep time: 10 minutes • **Total time:** 35 minutes, plus cooling • **Makes:** 16 blondies

1 cup (125g) all-purpose flour

½ tsp baking powder

⅛ tsp baking soda

¼ tsp salt

5 tbsp salted butter, melted

¾ cup (150g) light brown sugar

¼ cup (50g) granulated sugar

1 egg

2 tsp vanilla extract

¾ cup (135g) white chocolate chips

½ cup (65g) macadamia nuts

1   Preheat the oven to 350°F (175°C). Line the bottom and sides of an 8 x 8-in (20 x 20cm) baking pan with aluminum foil, leaving an overhang on all sides.

2   In a medium bowl, whisk the flour, baking powder, baking soda, and salt together. Set aside.

3   In a large bowl, whisk together the melted butter, brown sugar, and granulated sugar. Add the egg and vanilla extract, whisking vigorously until combined. Slowly add the flour mixture into the wet ingredients, stirring with a large spoon or rubber spatula until combined. Do not overmix. The batter will be thick. Fold in most of the white chocolate chips and macadamia nuts, leaving just 1 tablespoon of each aside.

4   Pour the batter into the prepared baking pan. Sprinkle with the reserved white chocolate chips and macadamia nuts. Bake for 25 minutes, or until light golden brown on top. Allow the blondies to cool completely in the pan on a wire rack. Once they have cooled, lift the foil out of the pan using the overhang on the sides and cut into squares. The blondies will stay fresh in an airtight container at room temperature for 1 week.

CINNAMON ROLL BLONDIES

I don't think there is anything more comforting than the scent of freshly baked cinnamon rolls wafting through the kitchen, so I replicated everything I love about cinnamon rolls into a quick and easy little dessert. These blondies use the same base recipe as my White Chocolate Macadamia Nut Blondies (page 47), but the simple addition of nutmeg and cinnamon gives them that wonderful aroma. Each buttery, dense blondie is topped with vanilla glaze, making them completely irresistible. This is the perfect recipe if you don't have the patience for a yeast dough and you want a cinnamon roll right now!

Prep time: 15 minutes • **Total time:** 40 minutes, plus cooling • **Makes:** 16 blondies

BLONDIES

1 cup (125g) all-purpose flour

½ tsp baking powder

⅛ tsp baking soda

¼ tsp salt

1¼ tsp ground cinnamon

pinch ground nutmeg

5 tbsp salted butter, melted

¾ cup (150g) light brown sugar

¼ cup (60g), plus 1 tbsp granulated sugar

1 egg

2 tsp vanilla extract

VANILLA GLAZE

¾ cup confectioners' sugar, sifted

3 tsp milk

½ tsp vanilla extract

1. Preheat the oven to 350°F (175°C). Line the bottom and sides of an 8 x 8-in (20 x 20cm) baking pan with aluminum foil, leaving an overhang on all sides.

2. **MAKE THE BLONDIES:** In a medium bowl, whisk the flour, baking powder, baking soda, salt, 1 teaspoon of the cinnamon, and the nutmeg together. Set aside.

3. In a large bowl, whisk together the melted butter, brown sugar, and ¼ cup (60g) granulated sugar. Add the egg and vanilla extract, whisking vigorously until combined. Slowly add the flour mixture into the wet ingredients, stirring with a large spoon or rubber spatula until combined. Do not overmix. The batter will be thick.

4. Pour the batter into the prepared baking pan. In a small dish, mix the remaining ¼ teaspoon cinnamon and 1 tablespoon granulated sugar together. Sprinkle over the batter. Bake for 25 minutes, or until light golden brown on top. Allow the blondies to cool completely in the pan set on a wire rack.

5. **MAKE THE GLAZE:** While the blondies are cooling, mix all of the glaze ingredients together in a small bowl, making sure there are no lumps of confectioners' sugar. Drizzle the glaze over the cooled blondies.

6. Lift the foil out of the pan using the overhang on the sides and cut into squares. The blondies will stay fresh an airtight container at room temperature for 1 week.

DARK CHOCOLATE RASPBERRY CHEESECAKE BARS

Cheesecake is my obsession, and even though Kevin doesn't like it, I still make these bars all the time. Having all this cheesecake madness to myself is dangerous, but each creamy bite is so worth it. These decadent bars call for only eight easy ingredients, and the batter comes together in minutes. And get this: the crust is made from melted butter and Oreos®. If that doesn't make you get up and start making these, I don't know what will!

Prep time: 15 minutes • **Total time:** 50 minutes, plus cooling • **Makes:** 16 bars

CRUST

20 Oreo® cookies
(Double Stuf or regular)

5 tbsp butter, melted

FILLING

16oz (448g), cream cheese softened to room temperature

1 egg

¼ cup (50g) granulated sugar

2 tsp, vanilla extract

1½ cups (210g) fresh raspberries

⅓ cup (60g) dark chocolate chips

1   Preheat the oven to 350°F (175°C). Line the bottom and sides of an 8 x 8-in (20 x 20cm) or 9 x 9-in (23 x 23cm) baking pan with aluminum foil, leaving an overhang on all sides. Set aside.

2   **MAKE THE CRUST:** In a food processor or blender, pulse the whole Oreos® into a fine crumb. Stir the cookie crumbs and melted butter together in a medium bowl. Press into the lined pan and bake for 9–10 minutes. Allow to cool as you prepare the filling.

3   **MAKE THE FILLING:** Using a handheld or stand mixer fitted with a paddle attachment, beat the cream cheese, egg, granulated sugar, and vanilla together in a large bowl on medium speed until smooth and creamy, about 3 full minutes. Gently fold in the raspberries and ¼ cup (45g) of the dark chocolate chips. Spread the mixture over your cooled crust. Top with the remaining dark chocolate chips.

4   Bake for 30–35 minutes, or until the cheesecake has set and the edges are lightly browned. Allow to cool completely in the refrigerator for at least 3 hours. Lift the foil out of the pan using the overhang on the sides and cut into squares. These bars will stay fresh in an airtight container in the refrigerator for 5 days.

 SALLY SAYS: Sliced strawberries and white chocolate would make tasty substitutions for the raspberries and dark chocolate. I've made these bars with chopped Snickers® before too. They are one of the most popular recipes on my website!

SUGARED LEMON BARS

I once made these zesty dessert bars for a girls' night, and they were gone before I even poured myself a glass of wine. It's the combination of the buttery shortbread crust with the undeniably creamy lemon filling that makes each bite so irresistible. Finding the perfect balance of sweet and tart is tricky when it comes to lemon desserts, but this recipe nails it every time!

Prep time: 25 minutes • **Total time:** 55 minutes, plus cooling • **Makes:** 24 bars

Shortbread Crust

1 cup (230g) butter, melted

½ cup (100g) granulated sugar

2 tsp vanilla extract

½ tsp salt

2 cups (250g) all-purpose flour

Lemon Filling

2 cups (400g) granulated sugar

6 tbsp all-purpose flour

6 eggs

1 cup (240ml) fresh lemon juice

confectioners' sugar, for topping

1   Preheat the oven to 300°F (145°C). Line the bottom and sides of a 9 x 13-in (23 x 23cm) baking pan with aluminum foil, leaving an overhang on all sides. Set aside.

2   **MAKE THE CRUST:** Stir the melted butter, granulated sugar, vanilla, and salt together in a large bowl. Add the flour and stir until everything is combined. Press the mixture evenly into the prepared baking pan and bake for 20 minutes.

3   **MAKE THE FILLING:** While the crust is baking, whisk the sugar and flour together until thoroughly combined. Whisk in the eggs and lemon juice until well mixed. Remove the crust from the oven and pour the filling evenly on top. Bake the bars for 22–25 minutes, or until the center is set and doesn't jiggle. Remove from the oven and chill for at least 4 hours.

4   Lift the foil out of the pan using the overhang on the sides and cut into bars. Sprinkle each with confectioners' sugar. The bars will stay fresh in an airtight container in the refrigerator for up to 4 days. Serve chilled.

APPLE PIE STREUSEL BARS

Apple pie is a staple at our Thanksgiving table. While I don't mind getting my hands dirty and whipping up an apple pie from scratch, I find baking all the same flavors in bar form to be much easier. And quicker too! A plethora of cinnamon-spiced apples and a crumbly brown sugar streusel will have you yearning for those crisp fall days and cozy sweaters any time of the year.

Prep time: 25 minutes • **Total time:** 1 hour, 10 minutes, plus cooling and chilling • **Makes:** 12 bars

SHORTBREAD CRUST

½ cup (115g) butter, melted

¼ cup (50g) granulated sugar

1 tsp vanilla extract

¼ tsp salt

1 cup (125g) all-purpose flour

APPLE FILLING

2 large Granny Smith apples, peeled and thinly sliced ¼ in (6mm) thick

2 tbsp all-purpose flour

2 tbsp granulated sugar

1 tsp ground cinnamon

pinch ground nutmeg

STREUSEL

½ cup (40g) old-fashioned oats

⅓ cup (70g) dark brown sugar

¼ tsp ground cinnamon

¼ cup (30g) all-purpose flour

¼ cup (60g) butter, cold and cubed

1   Preheat the oven to 300°F (145°C). Line an 8 x 8-in (20 x 20cm) baking pan with aluminum foil, leaving an overhang on all sides. Set aside.

2   **MAKE THE CRUST:** Stir the melted butter, granulated sugar, vanilla, and salt together in a medium bowl. Add the flour and stir until everything is combined. Press the mixture evenly into the prepared baking pan. Bake for 15 minutes while you prepare the filling and streusel.

3   **MAKE THE APPLE FILLING:** Combine the sliced apples, flour, granulated sugar, cinnamon, and nutmeg together in a large bowl until all of the apples are evenly coated. Set aside.

4   **MAKE THE STREUSEL:** Whisk the oats, brown sugar, cinnamon, and flour together in a medium bowl. Cut in the chilled butter with a pastry blender or with your hands until the mixture resembles coarse crumbs. Set aside.

5   Remove the crust from the oven, and turn the oven up to 350°F (175°C). Evenly layer the apples on top of the warm crust. It will look like there are too many apple slices, so layer them tightly and press them down to fit. Sprinkle the apple layer with streusel and bake for 30–35 minutes, or until the streusel is golden brown. Remove from the oven and allow to cool for at least 20 minutes at room temperature, then chill in the refrigerator for at least 2 hours. Lift the foil out of the pan using the overhang on the sides and cut into bars. These can be enjoyed warm or cold. The bars will stay fresh in an airtight container in the refrigerator for 3 days.

 SALLY SAYS: Try substituting the apples for peaches in the summertime. Sometimes I add white chocolate chips or toffee bits to the streusel for a decadent treat.

SALTED CARAMEL CRISPY TREATS

This recipe was a happy accident. With a bowl of salted caramel left over from an apple recipe I was working on, I decided to swirl it into a pan of crispy treats to take to my neighbors. The result is the best thing to have ever happened to a crispy cereal square! Each bite is a cross between a bowl of salty caramel corn and gooey marshmallows. The fact that they take less than 15 minutes to make can be our little secret.

Prep time: 15 minutes • **Total time:** 15 minutes, plus cooling • **Makes:** 16 squares

¼ cup (60g) butter

1 x 10-oz (285g) bag large or miniature marshmallows

4½ cups (128g) puffed rice cereal

½ cup (105g) salted caramel sauce (page 91), divided

sea salt, to decorate

1   Lightly spray a 9 x 9-in (23 x 23cm) baking dish with non-stick cooking spray. Set aside.

2   Melt the butter in a medium saucepan over low heat. Add the marshmallows until they are just about fully melted into the butter—some chunks of marshmallow may remain. Remove from the heat and add the cereal. Stir until fully coated. Gently fold in half of the salted caramel sauce.

3   Spoon the mixture into the prepared baking pan and gently spread it out evenly. Drizzle with the remaining salted caramel sauce. Gently press the mixture down into the pan. Use the back of a large spatula sprayed with non-stick spray to prevent sticking when pressing into the pan. Sprinkle with sea salt. Allow to cool at room temperature for at least 1 hour before cutting. The squares will stay fresh in an airtight container at room temperature for 7 days.

 SALLY SAYS: The secret to soft and gooey crispy treats is to not pack the treats into your baking pan. Rather, you want to gently mold them into the pan's shape using the back of a spatula sprayed with non-stick spray.

SPICED PUMPKIN PIE BARS

I don't remember a single Thanksgiving holiday without a giant slice of Mom's homemade pumpkin pie. With a dollop of whipped topping, digging into that fat slice is always the best part of the day—no matter how stuffed I am. These creamy pumpkin bars are my take on Mom's classic. They're not overly sweet, so all you taste is pure pumpkin and its complementary spices. The cream cheese provides structure to the bars, but doesn't overpower the pumpkin flavor at all. In fact, my taste testers didn't even notice it!

Prep time: 15 minutes • **Total time:** 1 hour, 10 minutes, plus cooling • **Makes:** 16 bars

GRAHAM CRACKER CRUST

1½ cups (135g) graham cracker crumbs

6 tbsp butter, melted

⅓ cup (65g) granulated sugar

PUMPKIN FILLING

8oz (225g) full-fat cream cheese

½ cup (100g) granulated sugar

3 eggs

2 tsp vanilla extract

1¼ cup (285g) pumpkin purée

⅓ cup (80g) Greek yogurt
(or regular yogurt, plain or vanilla)

2 tsp ground cinnamon

½ tsp ground cloves

½ tsp ground nutmeg

whipped cream, for topping
(optional)

1   Preheat the oven to 325°F (160°C). Line the bottom and sides of an 8 x 8-in (20 x 20cm) or 9 x 9-in (23 x 23cm) baking pan with aluminum foil, leaving an overhang on all sides. Set aside.

2   **MAKE THE CRUST:** Mix the graham cracker crumbs, melted butter, and granulated sugar together in a medium bowl until combined. Press into the bottom of the prepared pan. The crust will be thick. Bake the crust for 10 minutes as you prepare the filling.

3   **MAKE THE FILLING:** Using a handheld or stand mixer fitted with a paddle attachment, beat the cream cheese and granulated sugar together in a large bowl on high speed until creamy, about 1 minute. On low speed, add the eggs one at a time, beating well after each addition. Add the vanilla, pumpkin, yogurt, cinnamon, cloves, and nutmeg. Beat until everything is combined and creamy. Pour the filling into the warm crust.

4   Bake for 40–45 minutes, making sure to loosely cover the bars with aluminum foil halfway through to prevent the top from getting too brown. The bars are done when the edges are lightly brown and the center is set. Allow to cool completely in the refrigerator for at least 3 hours. Lift the foil out of the pan using the overhang on the sides and cut into squares. The bars will stay fresh in an airtight container in the refrigerator for 5 days.

CAKES, PIES & CRISPS

While cakes, pies, and crisps are associated more with special occasions, there doesn't need to be a holiday approaching to enjoy any of the following recipes. I'll take a giant slice of triple-layer cake any day of the week!

Settling on only ten recipes for this chapter was challenging. There are so many immaculate options in the world of cakes, pies, and crisps: summery classics like peach and key lime pies; towering banana cake and super-moist peanut butter cake smothered in rich chocolate frosting; or cookie cheesecake, caramel, coffee, and vanilla beans galore. Yeah, the following pages include it all. You won't even need an oven for two of these mouthwatering recipes!

Most of the desserts in this chapter taste best served on the day they are made, although baked and frozen cakes can be made one day in advance and frosted or decorated immediately before serving if you want a delicious treat on standby.

FROZEN PEANUT BUTTER BANANA PIE

This no-bake pie is the answer to all of your peanut butter cravings. Made from homemade whipped cream, thick cream cheese, and a colossal amount of peanut butter, it's a smorgasbord of pure decadence. The ultra creamy peanut butter filling sits atop a thick Oreo® cookie crust and layers of sliced bananas. The best part is that you don't even need to turn on your oven. Let your freezer do all the work!

Prep time: 20 minutes • **Total time:** 30 minutes, plus 6 hours freezing • **Makes:** 1 pie

BASE

28 Oreo® cookies, crushed into crumbs

5 tbsp butter, melted

2 bananas, thinly sliced, plus more to decorate (optional)

FILLING

1 cup (240ml) heavy cream

8oz (225g) full-fat cream cheese

1 cup (250g) creamy peanut butter

½ cup (100g) granulated sugar

1 tbsp vanilla extract

1   **MAKE THE BASE:** Combine the crushed Oreos® and melted butter in a medium bowl. Press the mixture evenly into the bottom and up the sides of a 9-in (23cm) springform pan. Arrange the banana slices on top of the crust in an even layer. Set aside.

2   **MAKE THE FILLING:** Using a hand-held or stand mixer fitted with a whisk attachment, whip the cream in a medium bowl on high speed until stiff peaks begin to form, about 4–5 full minutes. Set aside.

3   Using a hand-held or stand mixer fitted with a paddle attachment, beat the cream cheese and peanut butter together in a large bowl until smooth. Beat in the granulated sugar and vanilla extract until combined. Using a rubber spatula, fold in the whipped cream.

4   Spread the peanut butter filling on top of the banana slices. Cover and freeze for about 6 hours, or until firm.

5   Before serving, allow the pie to sit at room temperature for 10 minutes. Top with additional banana slices if desired.

 SALLY SAYS: Feeling a little adventurous? Drizzle the pie with melted peanut butter and a sprinkle of chocolate chips.

SWEET PEACH PIE

Homemade pies can be tricky, but they don't have to be. If you want to learn how to make a perfect pie, this straightforward recipe will get you there. A mixture of butter and shortening makes the golden crust ultra flaky and tender. The juicy peach filling is slightly sweet and bubbles with cinnamon and nutmeg. One slice of this pie will have you wishing peach season would never end!

Prep time: 1 hour 30 minutes • **Total time:** 2 hours, 30 minutes, plus cooling • **Makes** 8–10 servings

CRUST

2½ cups (315g) all-purpose flour, plus extra for dusting

1¼ tsp salt

6 tbsp butter, chilled and cubed

¾ cup (154g) vegetable shortening, chilled

¾ cup (180ml) ice water

PEACH FILLING

8 ripe but firm medium-size peaches, peeled and cored

1 tbsp fresh lemon juice

½ tsp vanilla extract

⅔ cup (84g) all-purpose flour

1 cup (215g) plus 1 tbsp granulated sugar

1 tsp ground cinnamon

½ tsp ground nutmeg

½ tsp salt

1 tbsp butter, cut into small pieces

1 egg, beaten

1 **MAKE THE CRUST:** Whisk the flour and salt together in a large bowl. Using a pastry blender or your hands cut in the butter and shortening until the mixture resembles coarse meal. Slowly drizzle in the ice water as you stir with a large spoon. Transfer the dough to a floured work surface and, using your hands, fold the dough into itself until the flour is fully incorporated into the fats. The dough should come together easily but should not feel overly sticky. Divide the dough in half, shape into two balls and wrap in plastic wrap. Chill in the refrigerator for at least 1 hour.

2 **ROLL OUT THE DOUGH:** On a floured work surface, roll out one of the balls of chilled dough (keep the other one in the refrigerator). Turn the dough about a quarter turn after every few rolls until you have a circle 12in (30cm) in diameter. Carefully place the dough into a 9 x 2-in (23 x 5cm) pie dish, and tuck it in with your fingers, making sure it is smooth. With a small and sharp knife, trim the extra overhang of crust and discard.

3 **MAKE THE FILLING:** Cut the peaches into ¼-in-thick (6mm) slices. Mix them with the lemon juice and vanilla in a large bowl. In a separate bowl, whisk the flour, 1 cup (215g) of sugar, cinnamon, nutmeg, and salt together until no large flour lumps remain. Add to the peaches and mix until combined. Pour the filling into the crust. Top with pieces of butter.

4 Adjust the oven rack to the lower third position and preheat the oven to 450°F (235°C).

5 **MAKE THE LATTICE TOP CRUST:** Remove the other ball of chilled dough from the refrigerator. Roll the dough out into a circle 10in (25cm) in diameter. Using a pastry wheel, sharp knife, or pizza cutter, cut 16 strips ½ in (13mm) wide. Carefully thread the strips over and under one another on top of the pie, pulling back strips as necessary to weave. Using a small and sharp knife, trim the extra overhang. Clamp down the edges of the dough with a fork or your fingers.

6 Lightly brush the lattice top with the beaten egg and sprinkle with 1 tablespoon of sugar. Place the pie onto a large baking sheet and bake for 10 minutes. Keeping the pie in the oven, lower the temperature to 350°F (175°C) and bake for an additional 45–50 minutes. If the crust is getting too brown too soon, cover loosely with aluminum foil and rotate the pie every 10 minutes. Remove the pie from the oven and allow to cool in the pan on a wire rack for at least 1 hour. The pie will stay fresh, covered, at room temperature for up to 2 days or in the refrigerator for up to 5 days. Serve the pie warm or chilled.

BROWN SUGAR MARBLE POUND CAKE

This is my "accidental" brown sugar pound cake. You see, the first few times I baked it, I found the texture a little too dry. I revamped the recipe adding more brown sugar and replacing butter with oil. It turned out to be one of the best pound cake decisions in the world! The result is one intensely rich cake with a tight, dense crumb. The vanilla and chocolate batters are made from the same brown sugar base, so it's an easy dessert to throw together. My favorite part is cutting into that first slice and unveiling the beautiful chocolate swirls!

Prep time: 15 minutes • **Total time:** 1 hour, 35 minutes • **Makes:** 1 pound cake

4 eggs

1 cup (200g) granulated sugar

1 cup (200g) light brown sugar

1 cup (240ml) milk

1 cup (240ml) vegetable oil

1 tbsp vanilla extract

seeds scraped from ½ vanilla bean

2 cups (250g) all-purpose flour

2 tsp baking powder

¼ tsp salt

3 tbsp unsweetened cocoa powder

1. Adjust the oven rack to the lower third position and preheat the oven to 350°F (175°C). Spray a 9 x 5-in (23 x 13cm) loaf pan with non-stick spray. Set aside.

2. In a medium bowl, whisk the eggs, granulated sugar, and brown sugar together until combined. Whisk in the milk, oil, vanilla, and vanilla seeds. Set aside.

3. In a large bowl, toss the flour, baking powder, and salt together. Pour the wet ingredients into the dry ingredients and whisk until just combined. Do not overmix.

4. Remove 1 cup (240g) of the batter and pour into a small bowl. Stir in the cocoa powder. Pour one-third of the vanilla batter into the prepared loaf pan. Spoon one-third of the chocolate batter on top. Repeat until both batters are gone. Gently swirl a large knife through the batter, making rounded horizontal zigzags from one side of the pan to the other. Wipe the excess batter from the knife. Repeat the swirling pattern in the opposite direction.

5. Bake for 60–70 minutes, making sure to loosely cover the cake with aluminum foil halfway through to prevent the top from getting too brown. The loaf is done when a toothpick inserted in the center comes out practically clean with only a few moist crumbs. Remove from the oven and allow the cake to cool completely in the pan set on a wire rack before removing and slicing. The cake will stay fresh, covered, at room temperature for up to 4 days.

 SALLY SAYS: This pound cake is absolute perfection topped with a simple melted chocolate drizzle, brown sugar glaze (page 2) or even salted caramel (page 91).

SALLY SAYS:

Buttermilk works its tangy magic to make this banana cake ultra soft and moist. I rarely have a carton of buttermilk in the refrigerator, so I often make my own. For this recipe, simply measure ½ tablespoon of lemon juice or white vinegar and add to a measuring glass. Add enough milk in the same measuring glass to reach ½ cup (120ml). Stir and let sit for 5 minutes. The homemade "buttermilk" will be somewhat curdled and ready to use.

BANANA CHOCOLATE CHIP LAYER CAKE

This cake is a tried-and-true crowd pleaser! How can it not be? The combination of bananas and chocolate is divine, and while it may look fancy, the batter comes together in a snap. The frosting on top is my all-time favorite milk chocolate frosting. It's featured on my blog, *Sally's Baking Addiction*, and readers frequently tell me it's the best frosting they've ever had!

Prep time: 20 minutes • **Total time:** 55 minutes, plus cooling • **Makes:** 12–14 servings

CAKE

½ cup (115g) butter, softened to room temperature

½ cup (100g) light or dark brown sugar

¾ cup (150g) granulated sugar

3 eggs, room temperature

1½ cups (340g) mashed banana (about 3 large very ripe bananas)

2 tsp vanilla extract

2 cups (250g) all-purpose flour

1 tsp baking soda

½ tsp ground cinnamon

1 tsp salt

½ cup (120ml) buttermilk (see *Sally Says*, opposite page)

1 cup (180g) mini or regular-size chocolate chips

MILK CHOCOLATE FROSTING

1¼ cups (290g) butter, softened to room temperature

3–4 cups (375–500g) confectioners' sugar

¾ cup (95g) unsweetened cocoa powder

3–5 tbsp heavy cream (or half-and-half)

1 tsp vanilla extract

¼ tsp salt

1. Adjust the oven rack to the lower third position and preheat the oven to 350°F (175g).

2. Generously coat two 9 x 9 x 2-in (23 x 23 x 5cm) round baking pans with non-stick cooking spray. Set aside.

3. **MAKE THE CAKE:** Using a handheld or stand mixer fitted with a paddle attachment, beat the butter, brown sugar, and granulated sugar together in a large bowl on medium speed until creamed, about 2–3 minutes. Add the eggs, one at a time, beating well on low speed after each addition. Add the mashed bananas and vanilla, beating on low speed for about 1 minute.

4. Whisk the flour, baking soda, cinnamon, and salt together in a medium bowl. Slowly add the dry ingredients to the wet ingredients in three additions, stirring by hand after each one. Add the buttermilk and stir until combined. The batter will be lumpy. Fold in the chocolate chips.

5. Divide the batter evenly into the prepared cake pans. Bake side by side until a wooden toothpick inserted in the center of the cakes comes out clean, about 22–24 minutes. Allow to cool completely in the pans set on a wire cooling rack.

6. **MAKE THE FROSTING:** Using a handheld or stand mixer fitted with a paddle attachment, beat the butter in a medium bowl on medium speed for 3–4 minutes. Add 3 cups (375g) of confectioners' sugar and cocoa powder. Mix on low. Add 3 tablespoons of heavy cream and the vanilla extract. If the frosting is too thin, add more confectioners' sugar (up to 1 cup or 125g), until you get the desired consistency. If the frosting is too thick, you can add more heavy cream (up to 2 tablespoons). Add the salt. If the frosting is still too sweet, add a dash more salt.

7. **ASSEMBLE THE CAKE:** Place a layer, flat side up, on a plate or cake stand. With a knife or offset spatula, spread the frosting over the flat side. Place the second layer on top, rounded side up, and spread the frosting evenly on the top and sides of the cake. Cover the cake and store at room temperature up to 4 days or in the refrigerator for up to 6.

VANILLA BEAN CAKE WITH STRAWBERRY WHIPPED CREAM

We make fresh strawberry whipped cream quite often around here. I love it as a topping for cupcakes, strawberry shortcake, and fresh fruit. But my all-time favorite dessert for this fluffy whipped cream is on top of a moist three-layer vanilla cake with a sweet strawberry jam in the middle. Don't let its elegance fool you; this stacked cake is an easy and impressive dessert to throw together for company!

Prep time: 25 minutes • **Total time:** 1 hour, 15 minutes, plus cooling • **Serves:** 12–16

FILLING

3 cups (375g) finely diced strawberries (about 15 medium strawberries), plus extra, sliced, to decorate (optional)

¾ cup (150g) granulated sugar

3 tbsp cornstarch

CAKE

3¼ cups (405g) all-purpose flour

1 tsp baking powder

½ tsp baking soda

1 tsp salt

1 cup (230g) butter

1¾ cups (350g) granulated sugar

2 eggs

½ cup (120g) Greek or regular yogurt (plain or vanilla)

1½ cups (360ml) milk

2 tsp vanilla extract

seeds scraped from 1 vanilla bean

STRAWBERRY WHIPPED CREAM

1½ cups (360ml) heavy whipping cream

3 tbsp granulated sugar

1½ tsp vanilla extract

1. Adjust the oven rack to the lower third position and preheat the oven to 350°F (175°C) degrees. Generously coat three 9 x 9 x 2-in (23 x 23 x 2cm) round baking pans with non-stick cooking spray. Set aside.

2. **MAKE THE FILLING:** Warm the diced strawberries in a small saucepan over a medium heat. Stir constantly for 4 minutes until the strawberry juices have been released. Add the granulated sugar and cornstarch and continue to stir for another 2 minutes. The mixture will thicken. Remove from the heat and allow to cool as you make the cake. The consistency of the filling should resemble spreadable jam.

3. **MAKE THE CAKE:** Whisk the flour, baking powder, baking soda, and salt together in a large bowl. Set aside. Melt the butter and place in a large bowl. Vigorously whisk in the granulated sugar, then the eggs, yogurt, milk, vanilla extract, and vanilla seeds until combined. Slowly whisk the wet ingredients into the dry ingredients until very few lumps remain. The batter will be extremely thick; do not overmix.

4. Divide the batter evenly between the three prepared cake pans. Bake for 20–22 minutes, making sure to loosely cover the cakes with aluminum foil halfway through to prevent the tops from getting too brown. The cakes are done when a toothpick inserted into the center comes out clean. Allow to cool completely in the pans set on a wire rack.

5. **MAKE THE WHIPPED CREAM:** Using a hand-held or stand mixer fitted with a whisk attachment, whip the cream, granulated sugar, and vanilla extract together in a medium bowl on high speed until stiff peaks begin to form, about 4–5 full minutes. Add ½ cup (70g) of the cooled strawberry filling and continue to beat for another 30 seconds.

6. **ASSEMBLE THE CAKE:** Trim the domed tops off the cakes with a large serrated knife. Place 1 layer on a plate or cake stand. With a knife or offset spatula, spread the top with half of the remaining strawberry filling. Repeat with the second layer and the rest of the strawberry filling. Place the third layer on top and spread the whipped cream evenly on the top and sides of the cake. There may be whipped cream left over, depending how thick you pile it on. Decorate with sliced strawberries if desired. Cover the cake and store in the refrigerator for up to 4 days.

DARK CHOCOLATE PEANUT BUTTER CAKE

I could make this peanut butter cake in my sleep. It's the recipe I turn to when I'm craving pure peanut butter and chocolate. Which, let's face it, is all the time. It's simply the moistest peanut butter cake I've ever eaten, and you won't be disappointed by the deep, decadent, and completely sinful dark chocolate frosting. If you like intensely flavored chocolate treats, this frosting is for you. Don't forget to decorate your cake with melted peanut butter and candies. You'll thank me later.

Prep time: 20 minutes • **Total time:** 55 minutes, plus cooling • **Makes:** 8–10 servings

Peanut Butter Cake

½ cup (115g) butter, softened to room temperature

¾ cup (150g) dark brown sugar

2 eggs

⅔ cup (170g) creamy peanut butter

1 tsp vanilla extract

1¼ cups (160g) all-purpose flour

1 tsp baking powder

¼ tsp salt

3 tbsp milk

Dark Chocolate Frosting

2¾ cups (330g) confectioners' sugar

⅔ cup (80g) unsweetened cocoa powder

6 tbsp butter, softened to room temperature

6 tbsp heavy cream

1 tsp vanilla extract

salt (optional)

½ cup (100g) Reese's Pieces®

¼ cup (60g) peanut butter for drizzling (optional)

1 Adjust the oven rack to the lower third position and preheat the oven to 350°F (175°C). Generously coat a 9 x 9 x 2-in (23 x 23 x 5cm) cake pan (or a 9-in or 23-cm springform pan) with non-stick cooking spray. Set aside.

2 **MAKE THE CAKE:** Using a handheld or stand mixer fitted with a paddle attachment, beat the butter and brown sugar together in a large bowl on medium speed until creamed, about 2–3 minutes. Add the eggs, one at a time, and beat until combined. Scrape down the sides of the bowl as needed. Add the peanut butter and vanilla extract and beat for 2 minutes. Set aside.

3 Whisk the flour, baking powder, and salt together in a medium bowl. Slowly add the dry ingredients to the wet ingredients in 3 additions, stirring by hand after each addition. The batter will be thick. Add the milk and mix until just combined; do not overmix.

4 Spoon the batter into the prepared cake pan. Bake for 32–35 minutes, making sure to loosely cover the cake with aluminum foil halfway through baking to prevent the top from getting too brown. The cake is done when a toothpick inserted in the center comes out clean. Allow to cool completely in the pan on a wire rack.

5 **MAKE THE FROSTING:** Sift the confectioners' sugar and cocoa powder together. Set aside. Using a handheld or stand mixer fitted with a paddle attachment, beat the butter in a medium bowl on medium speed until fluffy, about 2 minutes. Gradually add the sifted sugar/cocoa alternately with the heavy cream and vanilla. Beat on low speed after each addition. Adjust as needed—add more powdered sugar if the frosting is too dark for your taste, or add a pinch of salt if it is too sweet.

6 **ASSEMBLE THE CAKE:** Frost the cooled cake and decorate with Reese's Pieces®. For a peanut butter drizzle, melt the peanut butter in a small bowl for 20 seconds in the microwave. Using a spoon, lightly drizzle it over the top of the cake. Cover and store at room temperature up to 4 days or in the refrigerator for up to 6.

COOKIES 'N CREAM CHEESECAKE

Let's all agree that cookies 'n cream is one of the best ice cream flavors out there (in addition to mint chocolate chip, of course, page 151). I took everything I adore about that ice cream flavor—creamy texture, crunchy cookies, chocolate—and made one indulgent cheesecake. Each slice is served up on an Oreo® cookie crust with more crumbled Oreos® on top. This cheesecake will rock your cookie-loving world!

Prep time: 20 minutes • **Total time:** 1 hour, 20 minutes, plus overnight cooling • **Makes:** 12–14 servings

CRUST

20 Oreo® cookies (Double Stuf or regular)

5 tbsp butter, melted

FILLING

24oz (675g) cream cheese

1 cup (200g) granulated sugar

1 cup (240g) plain full-fat yogurt or sour cream

1 tbsp vanilla extract

3 eggs

18 Oreo® cookies (Double Stuf or regular), crumbled

whipped cream (optional)

1   Adjust the oven rack to the lower third position and preheat the oven to 350°F (175°C). Spray a 9-in (23cm) springform pan with non-stick cooking spray. Set aside.

2   **FOR THE CRUST:** In a food processor or blender, pulse the whole Oreos® into a fine crumb. Stir the cookie crumbs and melted butter together in a medium-sized bowl and press into the prepared pan. Wrap aluminum foil tightly around the outside walls of the springform pan. You'll see why in the next step. Bake for 9–10 minutes. Allow to cool as you prepare the filling.

3   **FOR THE FILLING:** Using a hand-held or stand mixer fitted with a paddle attachment, beat the cream cheese and granulated sugar together in a large bowl on medium speed until smooth and creamy, about 3 minutes. Add the yogurt and vanilla; mix well. On low speed, add the eggs one at a time, beating after each addition until just blended. Gently fold in 13 crumbled Oreo® cookies. Do not overmix. Pour the filling into the cooled crust. Place the springform pan into a large roasting pan and place into the oven. Fill the roasting pan halfway up with hot water. The foil wrapped around the sides of the springform pan will prevent water from leaking inside. The purpose of this "water bath" is to ensure even, gentle baking for the cheesecake.

4   Bake for 50–60 minutes, or until the center is almost set (see *Sally Says* below for more detail). Turn the oven off, and open the door slightly. Let the cheesecake sit in the oven for 1 hour. Remove from the oven and allow to cool completely at room temperature. Refrigerate for at least 4 hours or overnight. Loosen the cheesecake from the rim of pan and remove the rim. Crumble the 5 remaining Oreos® on top and garnish with whipped cream, if you like. Cut into slices and serve chilled. Cover the cake and store in the refrigerator for up to 4 days.

 SALLY SAYS: Avoid cracks in your cheesecake with these simple steps. 1) Be sure to mix the first four ingredients extremely well, eliminating all possible lumps in the cream cheese. 2) Eggs hold air inside the batter which could rise up and cause cracks, so mix the eggs as little as possible once you've added them. 3) Avoid overbaking! When the cheesecake is done, there will still be a 2- to 3-in (5 to 7cm) wobbly spot in the middle; the texture will smooth out as it cools.

KEY LIME PIE

This recipe is dedicated to my best friend, Amy. Amy loves key lime pie so much that it's her birthday cake of choice every year. And I personally love making this tangy pie because the ingredient list is so short! The graham cracker crust is extra thick and firm, providing a pleasant contrast in texture to the smooth and creamy filling. I add a bit of cream cheese to the filling so it remains sturdy and slightly firm when cut into slices. This is the best key lime pie—if you don't believe me, just ask Amy!

Prep time: 20 minutes • **Total time:** 40 minutes, plus chilling • **Makes:** 8–10 servings

GRAHAM CRACKER CRUST

1½ cups (135g) graham cracker crumbs

6 tbsp butter, melted

⅓ cup (65g) granulated sugar

FILLING

4oz (112g) full-fat cream cheese, softened to room temperature

4 egg yolks

14-oz (400g) can sweetened condensed milk

½ cup lime juice

zest of 1 lime

1 Adjust the oven rack to the lower third position and preheat the oven to 350°F (175°C). Spray a 9-in (23cm) pie dish with non-stick cooking spray. Set aside.

2 **MAKE THE CRUST:** Mix the graham cracker crumbs, melted butter, and granulated sugar together in a medium bowl until combined. Press into the bottom of the prepared pie pan and only slightly up the sides. The crust will be thick. Bake the crust for 12 minutes as you prepare the filling.

3 **MAKE THE FILLING:** Using a hand-held or stand mixer fitted with a paddle attachment, beat the cream cheese in a medium bowl on high speed until smooth, about 1 minute. Beat in the egg yolks, scraping down the sides as needed. Beat in the sweetened condensed milk, lime juice, and lime zest until combined. Pour into the warm crust.

4 Bake for 16–18 minutes, or until the sides are very lightly browned. The center may slightly jiggle, which is ok. Allow the pie to cool set on a wire rack for 30 minutes. Transfer to the refrigerator and chill for at least 4 hours before slicing. Serve the pie chilled. Cover the pie and store in the refrigerator for up to 3 days.

 SALLY SAYS: Make sure you use full-fat cream cheese and sweetened condensed milk in this recipe. Low-fat options don't allow the filling to set properly.

CARAMEL COFFEE CHOCOLATE CHIP TORTE

This decadent frozen dessert takes ice cream to a new level, and it couldn't be easier since the preparation time is only 15 minutes. I brought it along to a summer barbecue, and it disappeared before my eyes! One bite reminds me of my favorite frozen caramel coffee drink at the coffee shop. Drink your coffee and eat it too!

Prep time: 15 minutes • **Total time:** 15 minutes, plus 6 hours freezing • **Makes:** 12–14 servings

CRUST

28 Oreo® cookies, crushed into crumbs

5 tbsp butter, melted

FILLING

8-oz (225g) container Cool Whip®, thawed

1 quart (945ml) coffee ice cream, softened

⅓ cup (45g) chopped pecans

⅓ cup (60g) semi-sweet chocolate chips

⅓ cup (75ml) caramel sauce ice cream (for topping)

1 **MAKE THE CRUST:** Combine the crushed Oreos® and melted butter in a Medium bowl. Press the mixture evenly into the bottom and up the sides of a 9-in (23cm) springform pan. Set aside.

2 **MAKE THE FILLING:** In a large bowl, stir the frozen whipped topping and ice cream together until softened and combined evenly. Spoon the mixture into the prepared crust. Cover and freeze for about 6 hours or until firm.

3 Before serving, allow to sit at room temperature for 10 minutes. Top with pecans and chocolate chips. Drizzle with caramel sauce.

 SALLY SAYS: Avoid taking the torte on long trips, but to make it travel-safe on short hops, tightly pack it in a large cooler with ice packs to make sure it doesn't shift.

MIXED BERRY FRUIT CRISP

My mom is known for her incredible fruit crisps. Growing up, summertime meant playing by the pool by day and enjoying mixed berry fruit crisps by night. I happily gobbled up a serving or two, with a smile from ear to ear, each and every time! I could never quite figure out if I loved the fruity filling or the buttery oat topping more. When I began to make fruit crisps on my own, I made sure to include equal parts of both irresistible layers. Mixed berry is my favorite, but I use this recipe quite often in the fall with Granny Smith apples. It's lip smackin' good!

Prep time: 10 minutes • **Total time:** 55 minutes, plus cooling • **Serves:** 8–12

FILLING

5 cups (approx. 700g) mixed berries, such as blueberries, chopped strawberries, blackberries, and raspberries (fresh or frozen)

¼ cup (30g) all-purpose flour

1 cup (200g) granulated sugar

¼ tsp salt

juice of 1 lemon

½ tsp vanilla extract

TOPPING

¾ cup (150g) dark brown sugar

⅔ cup (85g) all-purpose flour

⅔ cup (65g) old-fashioned oats (or quick oats)

1 tsp ground cinnamon

¼ tsp salt

½ cup (70g) chopped pecans

½ cup (115g) butter, softened to room temperature

1 Preheat the oven to 350°F (175°C). Heavily coat a 9 x 9-in (23 x 23cm) baking pan with non-stick spray or butter. Set aside.

2 **FOR THE FILLING:** Combine 3 cups (420g) of the berries with the flour, sugar, salt, lemon juice, and vanilla in a large bowl. Toss to fully coat the berries in the mix. Spread them into the prepared baking pan. Top with the remaining berries.

3 **FOR THE TOPPING:** Whisk the brown sugar, flour, oats, cinnamon, salt, and pecans together in medium bowl. Make sure to get out all of the brown sugar lumps. Add the butter and stir with a rubber spatula or crumble with your hands until the mixture is crumbly.

4 Evenly sprinkle the topping over the filling. Bake for 40–45 minutes, until the topping is golden brown. Remove from the oven and cool slightly before serving. Cover the crisp and store at room temperature for 1 day or in the refrigerator for up to 5 days.

 SALLY SAYS: This fruity crisp can be enjoyed warm or cold. I personally love it warm with a big scoop of vanilla ice cream on top.

CANDY & SWEET SNACKS

I f you have more sweet teeth than you know what to do with, you're certainly going to enjoy the following chapter. My mind exploded with ideas to fill these pages, but I settled on a few crowd-pleasing favorites.

Most of the following recipes are perfect for gift giving. I like to arrange Marshmallow Swirl S'mores Fudge (page 84) and Pretzel Peanut Butter Cups (page 88) in parchment paper–lined gift boxes for friends. Who doesn't love receiving a box of homemade chocolate confections? Salty-sweet snacks such as Old-Fashioned Caramel Corn (page 94) and Monster Munch (page 95) travel well and can be mailed to all the lucky ones on your gift list.

The best part about this chapter? Most of the recipes are no-bake, so you can give your oven a break. From fudge to dip to truffles and pretzels, these are not your ordinary sugary sweets.

MARSHMALLOW SWIRL S'MORES FUDGE

My first camping experience included allergies, mosquitos, and shivering temperatures. Let's just leave it at that. The only good memory I have from the weekend is sinking my teeth into a few s'mores. I took my favorite part about camping and stuffed it into this creamy, silky fudge. Made from just a few ingredients, this low-maintenance fudge is worlds better than bug bites and sleeping bags if you ask me.

Prep time: 10 minutes ● **Total time:** 6 hours, 10 minutes ● **Makes:** 36 squares

2 cups (360g) semi-sweet chocolate chips

¼ cup (60g) butter

14-oz (400g) can full-fat sweetened condensed milk

2 cups (180g) mini marshmallows

4 full sheets graham crackers, broken into pieces

1   Line the bottom and sides of an 8 x 8-in (20 x 20cm) baking pan with aluminum foil, leaving an overhang on all sides. Set aside.

2   In a medium saucepan over a low-medium heat, combine the chocolate chips, butter, and sweetened condensed milk. Stir constantly until the chocolate chips are completely melted. The mixture will be very thick.

3   Remove from the heat and allow to slightly cool for 3–4 minutes. Gently fold in the marshmallows and graham cracker pieces. The marshmallows will melt slightly, creating swirls. Spoon the chocolate mixture into the prepared pan, smoothing down the top as best you can. Chill in the refrigerator for 4–6 hours, until firm. Using a very sharp knife, cut into squares.

4   Cover the fudge tightly and store in the refrigerator for up to 4 days.

 SALLY SAYS: This is my go-to chocolate fudge recipe. Instead of s'mores fixings, try adding walnuts, candy cane pieces, peanut butter swirls, or crushed Oreo® cookies.

MINT CHOCOLATE CHIP COOKIE DOUGH BITES

There are two types of people in this world: cookie people and cookie-dough people. I fall into the latter category. I've been caught with my finger in the cookie dough bowl one too many times, so I decided to make a recipe for all of us cookie-dough-crazed fans. Instead of the traditional chocolate chip, I stuffed these egg-free balls of dough with mint chocolate pieces and added a touch of peppermint extract. I'm going to warn you now: these addictive bites are hard to share!

Prep time: 30 minutes • **Total time:** 40 minutes • **Makes:** 40 bites

½ cup (115g) butter, softened to room temperature

¾ cup (150g) light brown sugar

2 tbsp milk or cream

1 tsp vanilla extract

dash peppermint extract

1¼ cups (160g) all-purpose flour

pinch salt

1½ cups (270g) Andes de Menthe® baking pieces or chopped Andes Thins

6oz (170g) coarsely chopped semi-sweet chocolate for drizzling, such as Baker's brand

1. Line a large cookie sheet with parchment paper or a silicone baking mat. Set aside.

2. In a large bowl using a handheld or stand mixer with a paddle attachment, beat the butter and brown sugar together on medium speed until light and creamy. Add the milk, vanilla, and peppermint extract and mix until combined. Turn the mixer off and add the flour and salt. Mix on low speed at first, then turn the mixer up to medium speed and mix until combined. The dough will be thick and crumbly, just keep mixing until it comes together. Stir in the Andes pieces.

3. Roll the dough into balls, about 1 teaspoon of dough per ball, and place them on the prepared cookie sheet. Place in the refrigerator to chill for a minute as you make the chocolate drizzle.

4. Melt the semi-sweet chocolate in a small microwave-safe bowl in 20-second increments until melted, stirring well after each increment. Remove the cookie dough from the refrigerator and drizzle the melted chocolate over each ball. Refrigerate the balls for at least 10 minutes to allow the chocolate to set. These bites remain fresh in an airtight container for up to 7 days.

 SALLY SAYS: There are two methods to melt chocolate: microwave or a double broiler. I prefer the microwave because it is easier. You just have to watch the chocolate very closely and stir it often to prevent it from seizing. Only a couple of extra seconds and you'll have burnt chocolate.

PRETZEL PEANUT BUTTER CUPS

Does it really get any better than a good ole peanut butter cup? Yes, it does. Make them with darker semi-sweet chocolate and add a crunchy, salty pretzel on top. Prepare to be amazed. I recently made homemade peanut butter cups for a bake sale. One happy buyer told me that she likes to sandwich mini Reese's cups between two pretzel twists. I instantly had an "aha! moment" and these sinful treats were born. Do yourself a favor and double this recipe. Twelve disappear quickly!

Prep time: 20 minutes • **Total time:** 20 minutes, plus 1 hour chilling • **Makes:** 12 cups

½ cup (125g) creamy peanut butter

2 tbsp butter, softened to room temperature

2 tbsp light brown sugar

½ cup (60g) confectioners' sugar

20oz (565g) coarsely chopped semi-sweet chocolate, such as Baker's brand

1 tsp shortening

Pretzels, optional

1   Line a 12-count muffin pan with cupcake liners. Set aside.

2   Using a hand-held mixer or stand mixer fitted with a paddle attachment, cream the peanut butter and butter together in a medium bowl on medium speed for 1 minute. Add the brown sugar and confectioners' sugar. Beat until combined and smooth. Place in the refrigerator until ready to use.

3   Melt the chocolate and shortening together in a medium microwave-safe bowl in 20-second increments until melted, stirring well after each increment. Spoon 2 teaspoons of melted chocolate into each of the cupcake liners. To allow the chocolate to settle evenly inside, bang the muffin pan against the counter a few times. Spoon 2 heaping teaspoons of the peanut butter mixture on top of the chocolate. Bang the pan on the counter or spread with a knife. If you want a traditional-looking peanut butter cup where the peanut butter layer isn't exposed on the sides, don't allow the peanut butter to reach the edges of the cup.

4   Spoon the remaining chocolate evenly on top of the peanut butter. Once again, bang the pan on the counter until the tops are smooth. If you'd like, affix a pretzel in the center of the chocolate top, and chill in the refrigerator for at least one hour. Cups stay fresh stored in an airtight container in the refrigerator for up to 7 days.

 SALLY SAYS: For a milder and sweeter chocolate coating, try using milk chocolate or white chocolate instead of semi-sweet. Crunchy or homemade/natural peanut butter may be used as well. You could also make 24–30 smaller peanut butter cups in a mini-muffin pan.

SALTED CARAMEL CHEESECAKE DIP

This thick and creamy dip is what I make when I need a knockout dish to take to a party. No one suspects how easy it is because they are too busy crowding the bowl. You'll only need three simple ingredients and a few dipping vehicles like graham crackers, pretzels, pita chips, and apples. The hardest part? Making sure you have enough left to bring along with you. It's impossible not to taste-test this stuff—repeatedly.

Prep time: 5 minutes • **Total time:** 5 minutes • **Makes:** about 2 cups (164g)

16oz (450g) cream cheese, softened to room temperature

⅔ cup (200g) room temperature salted caramel sauce (see recipe below)

⅓ cup (65g) dark brown sugar

1   Using a handheld or stand mixer fitted with a paddle attachment, beat the cream cheese on medium speed in a medium bowl until smooth and creamy, about 1 minute. Add the salted caramel and brown sugar and continue to beat until smooth and combined. Drizzle a few more drops of salted caramel sauce on top and gently swirl with a knife, if desired.

2   Cover the dip tightly and store in the refrigerator until ready to serve. This dip may be made 1 day in advance.

SALTED CARAMEL SAUCE

Salt and caramel come together in delicious harmony to make what I can only describe as … heaven. Homemade caramel is surprisingly simple to make as long as you plant yourself near the stove and continue to stir as the sugar melts down. I use this salted caramel in several recipes, including Salted Caramel Crispy Treats (page 56) and Apple Spice Cupcakes with Salted Caramel Whipped Cream (page 148), but feel free to drizzle over ice cream, cake, brownies, cookies, or even hot chocolate!

Prep time: 10 minutes • **Total time:** 10 minutes • **Makes:** 1 cup (210g)

1 cup (200g) granulated sugar

6 tbsp salted butter, cut into 6 pieces

½ cup (120 ml) heavy cream

1 teaspoon salt

1   Heat the granulated sugar in a medium saucepan over medium heat, stirring constantly with a rubber spatula. Sugar will form clumps and eventually melt into a thick brown liquid as you continue to stir. Be careful not to burn. Once melted completely, immediately add the butter. The mixture will bubble rapidly. Continue to stir for 2–3 minutes until the butter is completely melted. Stir in the heavy cream and allow to boil for 1 minute. Remove from heat and stir in the salt. Allow caramel to cool completely and thicken before using.

2   Store in the refrigerator in an airtight container for up to 1 month.

WHITE CHOCOLATE SWIRL BARK

Think of bark as your inner chocoholic's blank canvas. The sky is the limit! Instead of settling on one type of chocolate, I love to swirl two together. Creating the two-toned appearance is as easy as a few strokes with a knife or toothpick. There's no need to be neat and precise; the unique pattern is part of its charm. Decorating the top with festive colored goodies makes this bark a perfect homemade holiday gift.

Prep time: 10 minutes • **Total time:** 10 minutes, plus 20 minutes chilling **Makes:** about 1¼ pounds (568g)

10oz (280g) semi-sweet chocolate, such as Baker's brand

10oz (280g) white baking chocolate

⅓ cup (40g) dried cranberries

⅓ cup (40g) chopped pistachios

1   Line a large cookie sheet with parchment paper or a silicone baking mat. Set aside.

2   Melt the chocolates separately in two microwave-safe bowls or glass measuring cups in 20-second increments until melted, stirring well after each increment. White chocolate will seize quicker than semi-sweet chocolate, so be sure to watch it very carefully.

3   Pour the semi-sweet chocolate into an even layer on top of the prepared cookie sheet. Top with the white chocolate. Gently swirl with a sharp knife or toothpick. Top with dried cranberries and pistachios. Chill until set, about 20 minutes. Break into pieces. Keep the bark in the refrigerator, covered, for up to 7 days.

OLD-FASHIONED CARAMEL CORN

My grandma would be happy that her timeless caramel corn recipe is going into my cookbook. I have so many memories of sitting in her kitchen and watching the kernels pop as she mixed up the caramel. I can still hear that giant popcorn maker warming up! The sticky caramel sauce, made from a few simple ingredients, drenches every single kernel. Grandma made sure her caramel corn was easy to prepare so my sisters and I could help. We always doubled this recipe for our large family to enjoy around the holidays.

Prep time: 20 minutes • **Total time:** 1 hour, 20 minutes • **Makes:** 10 cups (500g)

10 cups (100g) air-popped popcorn

1 cup (200g) light brown sugar

¼ cup (80g) light corn syrup

½ cup (115g) butter

pinch cream of tartar

½ tsp salt

½ tsp baking soda

1 Preheat the oven to 200°F (95°C). Spread the popcorn out onto one or two large baking sheets. Set aside.

2 Combine the sugar, corn syrup, butter, cream of tartar, and salt in a medium saucepan over a medium-high heat. Stir constantly and bring to a boil for about 5 minutes. Remove from the heat and quickly stir in the baking soda. Pour the caramel over the popcorn and stir gently until all the kernels are coated.

3 Bake for 1 hour, stirring every 20 minutes. Allow to cool on the pan and break apart large clusters if desired. Cover the popcorn tightly once cooled; it will stay fresh for up to 2 weeks.

 SALLY SAYS: If you do not have a popcorn maker at home, you can simply add 3 tablespoons of popcorn kernels to a brown paper bag. Seal the bag tightly by folding over the top. Microwave the popcorn for approximately 1 minute, 45 seconds on high, or up to 2 minutes, depending on your microwave. This method will make 5 cups (50g).

MONSTER MUNCH

A giant bowl of snack mix can do no wrong, especially if it's drizzled with melted chocolate. I combine several favorites like honey roasted peanuts, homemade caramel corn, and crunchy pretzels to create one ultimate salty-sweet snack. The recipe makes a family-sized batch and is perfect for handing out at parties or to trick-or-treaters. But you might not have any leftover to give away—this stuff is so good, it's scary.

Prep time: 5 minutes • **Total time:** 25 minutes • **Makes:** about 10 cups (500g)

5 cups (250g) Old-Fashioned Caramel Corn (page 94)

3 cups (140g) pretzel twists

1 cup (200g) Reese's Pieces®

1 cup (125g) honey-roasted peanuts

4oz (113g) coarsely chopped semi-sweet chocolate, such as Baker's brand

1 Combine the caramel corn, pretzels, Reese's Pieces®, and peanuts together in a large bowl. Spread out onto two large cookie sheets. Set aside.

2 Melt the chocolate in a small microwave-safe bowl in 20-second increments until melted, stirring well after each increment. Drizzle the chocolate over the snack mix, then allow it to set for about 20 minutes before digging in. Cover the snack mix and store at room temperature for up to 2 weeks.

 SALLY SAYS: For easy drizzling, I use an old (and deeply cleaned!) plastic condiment bottle with a small spout. Melt the chocolate, pour it into the bottle, and neatly drizzle it over the snack mix. You can also use this bottle to drizzle the chocolate over Chocolate Glazed Orange Macaroons (page 121), Mint Chocolate Chip Cookie Dough Bites (page 87), or the glaze over Strawberry Rolls (page 23).

FUNFETTI CHEX MIX®

Some desserts are simply made to have fun while you eat. And this sweet Chex Mix® is a huge party in a bowl! Each cereal square tastes like funfetti cake, complete with a plethora of colorful sprinkles. I like to make this addicting little snack for every holiday, using different colored sprinkles. It takes minutes to throw together and even less time to gobble up!

Prep time: 10 minutes • **Total time:** 10 minutes • **Makes:** 6 cups (750g)

6 cups (150g) Rice Chex cereal

12oz (350g) white chocolate chips (or white candy melts or white almond bark)

1 tsp shortening

½ cup (80g) sprinkles

1 cup (140g) yellow or white boxed dry cake mix

½ cup (60g) confectioners' sugar

1 Pour the cereal into a very large bowl. Set aside.

2 Melt the white chocolate chips and shortening together in a medium microwave-safe bowl in 30-second increments until melted, stirring well after each increment. Be sure to watch it carefully, as white chocolate tends to seize quickly within seconds. Once melted and smooth, pour it over the cereal, stirring very gently to coat. You do not want to break up the cereal.

3 Pour the sprinkles, dry cake mix, and confectioners' sugar into a large zipped-top bag or large Tupperware® container. Add the cereal. Seal the bag or container and shake until all the cereal is coated with the powdered mixture. Discard any excess powder. Cover the snack mix and store at room temperature for up to 2 weeks.

CINNAMON-SUGAR SOFT PRETZELS

This basic soft pretzel recipe comes from Kevin's family. The first time we made them together, I was shocked by how easy they are to make! Simply mix the dough ingredients together, roll them up, drop into a baking soda bath, and bake. No mixer required, no waiting around for the dough to rise, and no endless kneading. They are incredible with a simple sprinkle of sea salt and a dunk in honey mustard, but my favorite topping is cinnamon sugar. Be sure to add the cinnamon sugar when the recipe states and not before baking, otherwise it will burn.

Prep time: 30 minutes • **Total time:** 45 minutes • **Makes:** 7–8 pretzels

PRETZELS

2¼ tsp instant dry yeast
(1 standard packet)

1½ cups (360ml) warm water
(approximately 110–115°F)

1 tsp salt

1 tbsp light brown sugar

4–4¼ cups (500–530g)
all-purpose flour, plus extra
for dusting

9 cups (2¼ L) water

⅔ cup (200g) baking soda

TOPPING

2 tbsp butter, melted

⅓ cup (40g) granulated sugar,
plus extra (optional)

1 tsp ground cinnamon, plus extra
(optional)

1 Preheat the oven to 425°F (235°C). Line two large baking sheets with parchment paper or silicone baking mats. Set aside.

2 Whisk the yeast with the warm water. Allow to almost fully dissolve, about 1 minute. Whisk in the salt and brown sugar until combined. Slowly add the flour 1 cup (125g) at a time. Mix with a large spoon until the dough is thick and no longer sticky. Do not add too much flour or the pretzels will not be soft. After 3–4 cups (375–500g) of flour, poke the dough with your finger—if it bounces back, it is ready to knead, if not, add a bit more flour.

3 Turn out the dough onto a floured surface. Knead the dough for 3 minutes and shape into a ball. With a sharp knife, cut it into 7–8 sections.

4 Roll each section into a 20-in (50cm) rope with an even diameter. Take the ends of the rope and form a giant U shape. Take the ends, twist them, and bring them in towards yourself to create a pretzel shape.

5 Whisk the water and baking soda together in a large pot. Bring to a boil. Place a pretzel onto a large slotted spatula and dip into the boiling water for 30 seconds. The pretzel will float. Lift the pretzel out of the water and allow the excess water to drip off. Place the pretzel onto the prepared baking sheet. Repeat with the rest of the pretzels.

6 Bake the pretzels for 10 minutes. Mix the granulated sugar and cinnamon together in a small bowl. Remove the pretzels from the oven and brush each top with the melted butter and generously sprinkle with the cinnamon sugar. Place back into the oven and bake for another 5 minutes. Remove from the oven and sprinkle with more cinnamon sugar, if desired.

7 Serve warm or at room temperature. Pretzels may be stored in an airtight container for up to 2 days. Pretzels freeze well, in a sealed container, for up to 2 months.

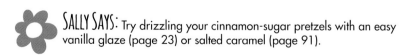 SALLY SAYS: Try drizzling your cinnamon-sugar pretzels with an easy vanilla glaze (page 23) or salted caramel (page 91).

COOKIES

Baking cookies fills your home with alluring smells, and it's one of the best ways to make friends and family feel welcome. Plus, there is just something about the taste of a fresh cookie that brings comfort and love. It's no wonder that they are the bread and butter of my blogging career! In fact, two of the recipes in this chapter have been featured in a magazine and another won a Nestlé® Toll House® baking contest.

I developed all the cookies in this chapter with the sole intention of creating recipes that are both easy and approachable. A few quick tips: Try to avoid overmixing your dough as this could lead to tough, hard cookies. You'll also notice that some recipes call for chilling your dough; cold dough will prevent the cookies from spreading in the oven, which is also why you should never put dough onto warm baking sheets. Sometimes I roll the dough into balls and then chill, and other times—if the dough is too sticky—I chill the dough as a whole and let it soften slightly before rolling into balls.

I favor soft, thick, and chewy cookies, and all of the following recipes will ensure yours come out the same way. If you like them a little crispier, simply bake each batch for a minute or two longer. To keep your cookies soft for days, store them in an airtight container with a piece of white bread. The cookies will absorb the bread's moisture. Most of the baked cookies can be frozen for up to 3 months and rolled cookie dough balls can be frozen for up to 2 months, unless otherwise noted.

So what are you waiting for? Go bake a batch and wait for all the smiles!

OATMEAL SCOTCHIES

Let's all agree that butterscotch deserves more attention. Those rich caramel notes combined with a buttery brown sugar taste, butterscotch will always be one of my favorite flavors. I left part of my test batch of these cookies with a friend and before I even got home, I received a text message saying that they were already gone! Be sure to use quick-cooking oats in this recipe, not whole-rolled oats. It's easy to get the two confused, but quick-cooking oats are more finely chopped and will mix into the dough more evenly.

Prep time: 15 minutes • **Total time:** 1 hour, 15 minutes • **Makes:** 30 cookies

1¾ cups (230g) all-purpose flour

1¼ tsp baking soda

½ tsp salt

1 tsp ground cinnamon

1 cup (230g) butter, softened to room temperature

½ cup (100g) granulated sugar

¾ cup (150g) dark brown sugar

2 eggs

2 tsp vanilla extract

3 cups (240g) quick-cooking oats

1¼ cup (225g) butterscotch chips

1 Whisk the flour, baking soda, salt, and cinnamon together in a large bowl. Set aside.

2 Using a hand-held or stand mixer fitted with a paddle attachment, cream the softened butter in a large bowl on medium speed, about 1 minute. Once creamy and smooth, add the granulated sugar and brown sugar. Beat on medium speed until fluffy and light in color. Beat in the eggs and vanilla extract, scraping down the sides of the bowl as needed. Set aside.

3 Slowly add the dry ingredients to the wet ingredients. Beat for 30 seconds until combined, then gradually tip in the oats. The dough will become quite thick, so finish mixing in the oats by hand with a rubber spatula or wooden spoon. Fold in the butterscotch chips. Cover and chill the dough for 30 minutes.

4 After 30 minutes, take the dough out of the refrigerator and allow to soften slightly at room temperature for 10 minutes.

5 Preheat the oven to 350°F (175°C). Line a large cookie sheet with parchment paper or a silicone baking mat.

6 Scoop the dough out of the bowl using a large cookie scoop or roll it into balls (about 2 tablespoons of dough per cookie). Arrange the balls 3in (7.5cm) apart on the cookie sheet and bake each batch for 8–10 minutes. The cookies will look very soft and underbaked. Remove from the oven and allow to cool on the sheet for 10 minutes before transferring to a wire rack to cool completely. The cookies will stay fresh in an airtight container at room temperature for up to 7 days.

 SALLY SAYS: I like to use a large cookie scoop when I make these oatmeal cookies. The dough is stiff and compact, so a cookie scoop makes the dough easier to align on the cookie sheet.

CHUNKY PEANUT BUTTER COOKIES

I'm a lifelong peanut butter lover. In fact, I have more peanut butter recipes on my website than any other ingredient. If you opened my cabinet, you would see about a dozen open peanut butter jars. Some might call it an obsession, but I just call it love. When I sat down to write this book, I knew I had to include the peanut butteriest cookie of all. An old-fashioned cookie with a modern twist. And it had to be soft! This cookie recipe is dedicated to all my fellow peanut butter lovers out there. You're not alone!

Prep time: 25 minutes • **Total time:** 2 hours, 50 minutes • **Makes:** 16 cookies

1¼ cups (160g) all-purpose flour

½ tsp baking powder

½ tsp baking soda

½ cup (115g) salted butter, softened to room temperature

¾ cup (150g) light or dark brown sugar

¼ cup (50g) granulated sugar

1 egg

1 tsp vanilla extract

½ cup (125g) crunchy peanut butter

⅔ cup (85g) salted peanuts or honey roasted peanuts

1 Whisk the flour, baking powder, and baking soda together in a large bowl. Set aside.

2 Using a handheld or stand mixer fitted with a paddle attachment, beat the butter, brown sugar, and granulated sugar together in a large bowl on medium speed until creamed, about 2–3 minutes. Add the egg and vanilla. Beat on medium speed for 1 minute, scraping down the sides as needed. Add the peanut butter and beat for 1 minute. Slowly add the dry ingredients into the wet ingredients using the mixer on low speed until combined. Do not over-mix. With a large spoon or rubber spatula, fold the peanuts into the dough. Cover the dough and chill for at least 2 hours (or up to 3 days).

3 Remove the chilled dough from the refrigerator and allow to soften slightly at room temperature for 10 minutes.

4 Preheat the oven to 350°F (175°C). Line two large cookie sheets with parchment paper or silicone baking mats.

5 Roll the dough into balls, about 2 tablespoons of dough each. Place on the cookie sheet about 3in (7.5cm) apart and, using a fork, lightly press down on the cookies, creating a criss-cross pattern on top.

6 Bake each batch for 12–13 minutes, until lightly browned on the edges. The cookies will look very soft and underbaked. Allow to cool on the cookie sheet for 10 minutes before transferring to a wire rack to cool completely. The cookies will stay fresh in an airtight container at room temperature for up to 7 days.

 SALLY SAYS: Making those iconic criss-cross patterns on top of these peanut butter cookies is much easier with chilled cookie dough; don't forget to let the dough chill for at least 2 hours in the refrigerator first.

CAKE BATTER CHOCOLATE CHIP COOKIES

If you want to know the most popular recipe on *Sally's Baking Addiction*, then look no further! These colorful cookies have been featured in *Woman's World* magazine and are loved by adults and children alike. I like to think of them as a scrumptious marriage between cake batter and chocolate chip cookie dough. Two of life's most guilty pleasures, indeed. The centers are soft, the edges are chewy, and the sprinkles are plentiful. While I love these cookies any day of the year, they taste especially wonderful for breakfast on your birthday … just saying!

Prep time: 20 minutes • **Total time:** 2 hours, 40 minutes • **Makes:** 24 cookies

1¼ cups (160g) all-purpose flour

1¼ cups (190g) yellow or white boxed dry cake mix

½ tsp baking soda

¾ cup (170g) butter, softened to room temperature

½ cup (100g) granulated sugar

½ cup (100g) light brown sugar

1 egg

1 ½ tsp vanilla extract

½ cup (90g) semi-sweet chocolate chips

½ cup (90g) white chocolate chips

½ cup (80g) sprinkles

1   In a large bowl, sift the flour, cake mix, and baking soda together. Set aside.

2   Using a handheld or stand mixer fitted with a paddle attachment, beat the butter, granulated sugar, and brown sugar together in a large bowl on medium speed until creamed, about 2–3 minutes. Add the egg and vanilla. Beat on medium speed for 1 minute, scraping down the sides as needed. Using the mixer on low speed, slowly add the dry ingredients into the wet ingredients until combined. Do not overmix. With a large spoon or rubber spatula, fold the chocolate chips, white chocolate chips, and sprinkles into the dough. Cover the dough and chill for at least 2 hours (or up to 3 days).

3   Remove the chilled dough from the refrigerator and allow to soften slightly at room temperature for 10 minutes.

4   Preheat oven to 350°F (175°C). Line two large cookie sheets with parchment paper or silicone baking mats.

5   Roll the dough into balls, about 1½ tablespoons of dough per cookie. Roll the cookie dough balls to be taller rather than wide. Place 3in (7.5cm) apart onto each cookie sheet and bake each batch for 10–12 minutes, or until the edges are slightly browned. The cookies will look very soft and underbaked. Remove from the oven and allow to cool on the cookie sheet for 5 minutes before transferring to a wire rack to cool completely. The cookies will stay fresh in an airtight container at room temperature for up to 7 days.

 SALLY SAYS: Dry cake mix is used to replace flour in this recipe to give the cookies their distinct "cake batter" taste. Make sure you sift the dry cake mix in with the flour and baking soda—cake mix tends to be lumpy, and the last thing you want are powdery lumps in your baked cookies. Trust me, it's not pretty!

GIANT OATMEAL RAISIN COOKIES

These may look like your average oatmeal raisin cookies, but don't be fooled—they are the best oatmeal cookies you'll ever make! It's a recipe for those of you who appreciate hearty, thick, and chewy oatmeal cookies. Loaded with cinnamon and raisins, they have been a hit from the first day I made them. I only use brown sugar to sweeten them, which leaves each cookie incredibly soft. A whopping ¼ cup (40g) of cookie dough goes into each rib-sticking cookie. Don't leave out the molasses—it gives these cookies an extra-dark, rich flavor.

Prep time: 10 minutes • **Total time:** 35 minutes • **Makes:** 12 large cookies

1⅔ cups (200g) all-purpose flour

1 tsp baking soda

½ tsp baking powder

½ tsp salt

1 tsp ground cinnamon

2 cups (160g) old-fashioned oats

1 cup (230g) butter, softened to room temperature

1½ cups (300g) dark brown sugar

2 eggs

1 tbsp dark molasses

2 tsp vanilla extract

1 cup (140g) raisins

1   Preheat the oven to 350°F (175°C). Line two large cookie sheets with parchment paper or silicone baking mats.

2   Whisk the flour, baking soda, baking powder, salt, and cinnamon together in a large bowl. Stir in the oats. Set aside.

3   Using a handheld or stand mixer with a paddle attachment, beat the butter and brown sugar together on medium speed in a large bowl until creamed—about 2–3 minutes. Add the eggs and mix until combined, scraping down the sides as needed. Add the molasses and vanilla and beat on medium speed for 2 minutes. Slowly add the dry ingredients into the wet ingredients using a mixer on low speed until combined. Do not overmix. With a large spoon or rubber spatula, fold the raisins into the dough. The dough will be heavy and sticky.

4   For each cookie, measure out ¼ cup (40g) of dough and shape it into a ball. Place 6 dough balls 4in (10cm) apart onto each cookie sheet.

5   Bake each batch for 12–13 minutes, until lightly browned on the edges. The cookies will look underbaked. Remove from the oven and allow to cool on the cookie sheet for 10 minutes before transferring to a wire rack to cool completely. The cookies will stay fresh in an airtight container at room temperature for up to 7 days.

RAINBOW CHOCOLATE CHIP COOKIES

The chocolate chip cookie is one of our household favorites. It's a timeless classic, an iconic dessert staple, and an unbeatable comfort food. Served warm, cold, dunked in milk, in dough form, in baked form, in ice cream, on ice cream, small, and large—few can resist the call of the chocolate chip cookie. And here is my favorite version, loaded with America's favorite colorful chocolate candy. The melted butter and extra egg yolk make the cookies extra chewy, but don't forget to chill the dough; it's the most important step!

Prep time: 15 minutes • **Total time:** 2 hours, 50 minutes • **Makes:** 16 large cookies

2¼ cups (280g) all-purpose flour

1 tsp baking soda

1½ tsp cornstarch

½ tsp salt

¾ cup (170g) butter, melted

¾ cup (150g) light brown sugar

½ cup (100g) granulated sugar

1 large egg, plus 1 egg yolk

2 tsp vanilla extract

½ cup (90g) semi-sweet chocolate chips

½ cup (85g) plain M&Ms®

1   Whisk the flour, baking soda, cornstarch, and salt together in a large bowl. Set aside.

2   In a medium bowl, whisk the melted butter, brown sugar, and granulated sugar together until no sugar lumps remain. Whisk in the egg, then the egg yolk, followed by the vanilla. Pour the wet ingredients into the dry ingredients and mix together with a large spoon or rubber spatula. Fold in the chocolate chips and M&Ms®. Cover the dough and chill for at least 2 hours (or up to 3 days).

3   Take the dough out of the refrigerator and allow to soften slightly at room temperature for 10 minutes.

4   Preheat the oven to 325°F (160°C). Line two large cookie sheets with parchment paper or silicone baking mats.

5   Roll the dough into balls, about 3 tablespoons of dough per cookie. If the dough is crumbly, the warmth of your hands will help it come together in a ball. Roll the cookie dough balls to be taller rather than wide. (See page VIII for a photo.) Place 8 balls of dough 3in (7.5cm) apart onto each cookie sheet.

6   Bake each batch for 11–12 minutes. The cookies will look very soft and underbaked. Remove from the oven and allow to cool on the cookie sheet for 10 minutes before moving to a wire rack to cool completely. The cookies will stay fresh in an airtight container at room temperature for up to 10 days.

 SALLY SAYS: I use this cookie dough base all the time and throw in everything from candy bars and nuts to dried fruits and even potato chips. Yes, potato chips! (page 113).

POTATO CHIP TOFFEE CHOCOLATE CHIP COOKIES

After one taste of these wacky cookies, you may never go back to an original chocolate chip cookie again! Crunchy, salty potato chips smother every chocolate-infused bite. The toffee chunks are buttery sweet, and the soft dough will melt in your mouth. One salty-sweet bite will satisfy every corner of your palate. These cookies are so tasty, they were even featured in *Woman's World* magazine! So if you're looking to break all the rules and give an unsuspecting chocolate chip cookie a flavor explosion, this is the perfect way!

Prep time: 15 minutes • **Total time:** 2 hours, 50 minutes • **Makes:** 16 large cookies

2¼ cups (280g) all-purpose flour

1 tsp baking soda

1½ tsp cornstarch

½ tsp salt

¾ cup (170g) butter, melted

¾ cup (150g) light brown sugar

½ cup (100g) granulated sugar

1 large egg, plus 1 egg yolk

2 tsp vanilla extract

½ cup (90g) semi-sweet chocolate chips

¾ cup (40g) crushed potato chips

½ cup (65g) toffee pieces (such as Heath® bars)

1 Whisk the flour, baking soda, cornstarch, and salt together in a large bowl. Set aside.

2 In a medium bowl, whisk the melted butter, brown sugar, and granulated sugar together until no sugar lumps remain. Whisk in the egg, then the egg yolk, and then whisk in the vanilla. Pour the wet ingredients into the dry ingredients and mix together with a large spoon or rubber spatula. Fold in the chocolate chips, potato chips, and toffee pieces. Cover the dough and chill for at least 2 hours (or up to 3 days).

3 Take the dough out of the refrigerator and allow to soften slightly at room temperature for 10 minutes.

4 Preheat the oven to 325°F (160°C). Line two large cookie sheets with parchment paper or silicone baking mats.

5 Roll the dough into balls, about 3 tablespoons of dough per cookie. If the dough is crumbly, the warmth of your hands will help it come together in a ball. Roll the cookie dough balls to be taller rather than wide. Place 8 balls of dough 3in (7.5cm) apart on each cookie sheet.

6 Bake each batch for 11–12 minutes. The cookies will look very soft and underbaked. Remove from the oven and allow to cool on the cookie sheet for 10 minutes before moving to a wire rack to cool completely. The cookies will stay fresh in an airtight container at room temperature for up to 10 days.

Freezing Cookie Dough

By freezing individual balls of dough you can make freshly baked cookies whenever the mood strikes. And if you're anything like Kevin and me, that will be pretty often!

1 Simply chill the cookie dough and portion it into balls.

2 Place the firm dough balls into a zip-top bag and freeze for up to 2 months. Mark the bag with the date, so you know when to discard.

3 To bake, simply place the frozen balls (do not thaw) on a cookie sheet and add 1 extra minute to the recipe's baking time.

SALTED CARAMEL DARK CHOCOLATE COOKIES

I like to call these my $5,000 cookies! Back in March 2013, I participated in a Nestlé® Toll House® baking contest against nine other fantastic food bloggers, and these dreamy dark chocolate cookies won first place! I've been making them for all the chocolate lovers in my life ever since because they are brownie-like cookies stuffed with gooey caramel and topped with sea salt. The most important step in making these little winners? Chill the cookie dough! Without chilling, it will be difficult to handle the sticky dough.

Prep time: 20 minutes • **Total time:** 2 hours, 50 minutes • **Makes:** 16 cookies

1 cup (125g) all-purpose flour

⅔ cup (80g) unsweetened cocoa powder

1 tsp baking soda

pinch salt

½ cup (115g) butter, softened to room temperature

½ cup (100g) granulated sugar

½ cup (100g) light or dark brown sugar

1 egg

1 tsp vanilla extract

2 tbsp milk

1½ cups dark chocolate chips (or semi-sweet)

18 chocolate-coated caramel candies, such as Rolo®

coarse sea salt

1   Whisk the flour, cocoa powder, baking soda, and salt together in a large bowl. Set aside.

2   Using a handheld or stand mixer fitted with a paddle attachment, beat the butter, granulated sugar, and brown sugar together in a large bowl on medium speed until creamed, about 2–3 minutes. Beat in the egg and vanilla extract. Scrape down the sides of the bowl as needed.

3   Slowly add the dry ingredients into the wet ingredients, and use a mixer on low speed until combined. Add the milk. With a large spoon or rubber spatula, fold the chocolate chips into the dough. The dough will be heavy and sticky. Cover and chill for at least 1–2 hours.

4   Take the dough out of the refrigerator and allow to soften slightly at room temperature for 10 minutes.

5   Preheat the oven to 350°F (175°C). Line two large cookie sheets with parchment paper or silicone baking mats.

6   Take 2 tablespoons of chilled dough, split it in half and roll each piece into a ball with your hands. Stick a caramel into 1 ball of dough. Top the caramel with the other ball of dough and seal down the sides so that the caramel is securely stuffed inside. Repeat with the rest of the dough and caramel candies. Place the balls 3in (7.5cm) apart onto each cookie sheet. Sprinkle each with sea salt before putting into the oven.

7   Bake each batch for 12–13 minutes. The cookies will appear undone and very soft. Allow to cool on the cookie sheet for at least 5 minutes before transferring to a wire rack to cool completely. The cookies will stay fresh in an airtight container at room temperature for up to 7 days.

 SALLY SAYS: The trick to stuffing the caramel candy inside is to make sure the dough completely envelops it, otherwise you'll have a leaking caramel mess on your cookie sheets!

MOM'S GINGERSNAPS

The smell of my mom's soft gingersnaps baking in the oven often greeted me when I got home from school during the winter. They were my favorite cookie growing up, and Mom knew just how excited I'd get right before I ate one, so she baked them often. Sometimes she'd wait for me to begin baking, and I got to roll the dough in the sugar… my favorite part! They're undeniably tender, chewy, and strongly spiced with ginger, molasses, cinnamon, and cloves. To get those iconic crinkles on top, be sure to press each cookie down gently with your fingers after you take them out of the oven.

Prep time: 10 minutes • **Total time:** 20 minutes • **Makes:** 24 cookies

2 cups (250g) all-purpose flour

2 tsp baking soda

1 tsp ground cinnamon

1 tsp ground cloves

1 tsp ground ginger

¾ cup (180ml) vegetable shortening

1⅓ cups (266g) granulated sugar

¼ cup (85g) dark molasses

1 egg

1 Preheat the oven to 350°F (175°C). Line two large cookie sheets with parchment paper or silicone baking mats. Set aside.

2 Whisk the flour, baking soda, cinnamon, cloves, and ginger together in a medium bowl until combined.

3 Using a handheld or stand mixer fitted with a paddle attachment, beat the shortening and 1 cup (200g) of the granulated sugar together in a large bowl on medium speed until creamed—about 2–3 minutes. Add the molasses and beat on medium speed for 1 minute. Add the egg and beat on medium speed for 1 minute, scraping down the sides as needed. Slowly add the dry ingredients to the wet ingredients using your mixer on low speed until combined. Do not overmix. The dough will be very thick and crumbly.

4 Pour the remaining sugar into a small bowl. Roll the dough into balls—about 1½ tablespoons of dough for each ball. The dough will be crumbly, but the warmth of your hands will help it come together in a ball. Roll each ball into the sugar. Place 2in (5cm) apart onto cookie sheets and bake for 8–10 minutes. The cookies will have spread only slightly, so press each cookie down gently with your fingertips to obtain the crinkled tops.

5 Allow to cool on the cookie sheet for 2 minutes before transferring to a wire rack to cool completely. The cookies will stay fresh in an airtight container at room temperature for up to 10 days (they won't last that long!).

 SALLY SAYS: Working with molasses can be a sticky situation! Always spray your measuring cup with non-stick cooking spray before adding the molasses. Why? If you don't, you'll be left with a sticky measuring cup and some of the molasses you need for the cookie dough will be stuck inside.

FROSTED SUGAR COOKIES

This is my favorite sugar cookie recipe—buttery, tender, soft, and sweet! They taste like those soft, frosted sugar cookies you can find in the grocery store's bakery, but without the long list of artificial ingredients. These are drop cookies, so there is no need to roll the dough out or cut it into shapes. The simple recipe means they're fun to make with kids around the holidays—or any time you need an extra sprinkle in your life!

Prep time: 15 minutes • **Total time:** 3 hours • **Makes:** 18–20 cookies

Sugar Cookies

1½ cups (190g) all-purpose flour

1 tsp baking powder

½ tsp baking soda

1 tsp cream of tartar

¼ tsp salt

½ cup (115g) butter, softened to room temperature

¾ cup (150g) granulated sugar

1 egg

2 tsp vanilla extract

Frosting

6 tbsp butter, softened to room temperature

2½ cups (300g) confectioners' sugar

1 tsp vanilla extract

3 tbsp heavy cream

pinch salt, as needed

sprinkles

1   **MAKE THE COOKIES:** Whisk the flour, baking powder, baking soda, cream of tartar, and salt together in a large bowl. Set aside.

2   Using a handheld or stand mixer fitted with a paddle attachment, beat the butter and granulated sugar together in a large bowl on medium speed until creamed, about 2–3 minutes. Add the egg and mix until combined, scraping down the sides as needed. Add the vanilla and beat on medium speed for 2 minutes. Slowly add the dry ingredients into the wet ingredients with your mixer on low speed until combined. Do not overmix.

3   Scoop out the dough, about 2 tablespoons of dough for each cookie, and roll into balls. Place the balls on a large plate and chill for at least 2 hours. This step will prevent the cookies spreading in the oven.

4   Preheat the oven to 350°F (175°C). Line two large cookie sheets with parchment paper or silicone baking mats. Place the chilled cookie dough balls onto the cookie sheet, about 3in (7.5cm) apart, and bake for 8 minutes. The cookies will look underbaked, but they will continue to bake on the cookie sheet as they cool. Remove from the oven and allow to cool on the cookie sheet for 10 minutes before transferring to a wire rack to cool completely before frosting.

5   **MAKE THE FROSTING:** Using a handheld or stand mixer fitted with a paddle attachment, beat the butter in a medium bowl on medium speed until fluffy, about 2 minutes. Switch to low speed and gradually add the confectioners' sugar. Beat for 1 minute. Add the vanilla and heavy cream and beat on medium speed for 2 minutes until combined. You can add more cream if the frosting is too thick or a pinch of salt if the frosting is too sweet.

6   Spread the frosting onto cooled cookies and decorate with sprinkles. They will stay fresh, covered, at room temperature for up to 2 days or in the refrigerator for up to 5. Unfrosted cookies may be frozen up to 3 months.

 SALLY SAYS: Try adding a few drops of liquid food coloring to the frosting and bring the festive cookies along to showers, birthdays, or holiday parties. You can also experiment with different extracts in the dough like almond, coconut, or lemon depending on your favorite flavors.

CHOCOLATE GLAZED ORANGE MACAROONS

Coconut macaroons are an oldie but goodie; a gold standard sought out by coconut lovers everywhere. This is my quick and easy recipe for coconut macaroons. Their toasty exterior combined with a chewy richness and moist center puts them at the top of my cookie list. I add a bit of orange zest to give each bite some summery zing. Chocolate is a necessary luxury I add at the last minute. After all, there is always room for a sweet chocolate drizzle!

Prep time: 10 minutes • **Total time:** 35 minutes • **Makes:** 15 cookies

MACAROONS

2¾ cups (200g) flaked/shredded coconut (sweetened)

⅔ cup (135g) granulated sugar

¼ cup (30g) all-purpose flour

¼ tsp salt

4 egg whites

½ tsp almond extract

1 tsp vanilla extract

zest of 1 large orange

CHOCOLATE GLAZE

3oz (75g) semi-sweet chocolate

¼ tsp shortening

1   Preheat the oven to 325°F (160°C). Line a large cookie sheet with parchment paper or a silicone baking mat. Set aside.

2   **MAKE THE MACAROONS:** In a large bowl, combine the coconut, sugar, flour, and salt. Add the egg whites and stir with a large rubber spatula until combined. Stir in the almond and vanilla extracts, then the orange zest.

3   Measure 1 heaping tablespoon of mixture for each and drop into a mound on the prepared cookie sheet, making sure they are nicely round and 2in (5cm) apart.

4   Bake for 20–22 minutes, or until the edges are lightly browned. Remove from the oven and allow to cool on the cookie sheet for 2 minutes, then transfer to a wire rack to cool completely.

5   **MAKE THE CHOCOLATE GLAZE:** Melt the chocolate and shortening together in a small microwave-safe bowl in 20-second intervals until melted, stirring well after each increment. Drizzle over the cookies. The macaroons will stay fresh in an airtight container at room temperature for up to 2 days or in the refrigerator for up to 5.

 SALLY SAYS: Instead of orange zest, try adding lemon zest with a drizzle of white chocolate to mix things up.

CINNAMON SPICE PUMPKIN OATMEAL COOKIES

Oatmeal cookies and pumpkin pie will be forever loved, so I decided to combine the two classics and create something using the best parts of each: the fabulous spice flavor of pumpkin pie and the soft, thick, and chewy texture of oatmeal cookies. What I love most is that they aren't cakey like a lot of pumpkin cookies, by skipping the eggs and getting as much moisture out of the pumpkin purée as possible. It really works!

Prep time: 20 minutes • **Total time:** 1 hour • **Makes:** 18 cookies

¾ cup (170g) pumpkin purée

2 cups (250g) all-purpose flour

1 tsp baking soda

2 tsp ground cinnamon

½ tsp ground nutmeg

½ tsp ground cloves

½ tsp ground ginger

½ tsp salt

1½ cups (120g) old-fashioned oats

1 cup (230g) butter, melted

¾ cup (150g) granulated sugar

½ cup (100g) light brown sugar

2 tsp vanilla extract

1 cup (240g) cinnamon chips

1   Line a small bowl with a paper towel. Spoon pumpkin purée on top, then press down. The point is to drain as much water out of the pumpkin purée as you can. Set drained pumpkin aside.

2   Whisk the flour, baking soda, cinnamon, nutmeg, cloves, ginger, salt, and oats together in a large bowl. Set aside.

3   In a medium bowl, vigorously whisk the melted butter, granulated sugar, brown sugar, and vanilla extract together until combined. Whisk in the pumpkin. The mixture will be thick. Pour the wet ingredients into the dry ingredients and mix together with a large spoon or rubber spatula. Fold in the cinnamon chips.

4   Place cookie dough in the refrigerator for about 5–10 minutes. If chilling for longer, make sure to let the cookie dough sit at room temperature to soften before rolling and baking.

5   Preheat the oven to 350°F (175°C). Line two large cookie sheets with parchment paper or silicone baking mats.

6   Take the dough out of the refrigerator. Scoop 2 tablespoons dough per cookie and roll into balls. Arrange the balls 3in (7.5cm) apart on the cookie sheet and slightly flatten each before baking. Flattening helps the cookies spread evenly as they bake.

7   Bake the cookies for 12–13 minutes, or until lightly browned on the sides. The cookies will be thick and look very soft in the centers. Allow to cool on the cookie sheets for 5 minutes before transferring to a wire rack to cool completely. The cookies will stay fresh in an airtight container at room temperature for up to 7 days.

 SALLY SAYS: Right when they come out of the oven, I like to press a couple of extra cinnamon chips into the tops of the warm cookies. This is just for looks, but don't they look pretty?!

CREAM CHEESE COOKIES 'N CREAM COOKIES

Okay, now we're getting out of control. After tasting these cookies, I'm convinced it doesn't get much better than adding chopped cookies . . . to cookies, so we're going to throw Oreos® into a simple, homemade cookie dough. Cream cheese is a secret ingredient lending the softest, creamiest texture ever. So think of these as the Cookies 'n Cream Cheesecake on page 74 in cookie form! As always, don't skip chilling the cookie dough.

Prep time: 20 minutes • **Total time:** 2 hours, 40 minutes • **Makes:** about 32 cookies

2¼ cups (280g) all-purpose flour

1 tsp baking soda

1 tsp cornstarch

¾ tsp salt

2oz (55g) cream cheese, softened to room temperature

½ cup (115g) butter, softened to room temperature

¾ cup (150g) light brown sugar

½ cup (100g) granulated sugar

2 eggs

1 tsp vanilla extract

8 Oreo® cookies (Double Stuf or regular), chopped into small pieces

1   Whisk the flour, baking soda, cornstarch, and salt together in a large bowl. Set aside.

2   Using a hand-held or stand mixer fitted with a paddle attachment, beat the cream cheese and butter together in a large bowl on high speed for 1 minute. Once creamy and smooth, add the brown sugar and granulated sugar. Beat on medium speed until fluffy and light in color. Beat in the eggs and vanilla extract, scraping down the sides of the bowl as needed.

3   Slowly add the dry ingredients to the wet ingredients with the mixer running on low speed. Continue to beat until everything is combined. Using a large spoon or rubber spatula, fold in the chopped Oreos®. Cover and chill the dough for at least 2 hours (or up to 3 days).

4   Take the dough out of the refrigerator and allow to soften slightly at room temperature for 10 minutes.

5   Preheat the oven to 350°F (175°C). Line two large cookie sheets with parchment paper or silicone baking mats.

6   Scoop 2 tablespoons dough per cookie and roll into balls. Place on the cookie sheet about 3in (7.5cm) apart.

7   Bake each batch for 10 minutes, or until the edges are lightly browned. The cookies will look very soft in the centers. Allow to cool on the cookie sheets for 5 minutes before transferring to a wire rack to cool completely. The cookies will stay fresh in an airtight container at room temperature for up to 7 days.

 SALLY SAYS: Pay attention to the bake time. You want to slightly underbake these cookies because they will continue to cook on the baking sheet when you remove them from the oven. 10 minutes is the sweet spot.

CHOCOLATE HAZELNUT SUPREMES

I usually make these chewy oatmeal cookies with peanut butter, but on a whim, I decided to give them a whirl with chocolate hazelnut spread instead. I'm not sure what inspired me, but it must have been the tempting jar of Nutella® that calls my name every time I open my pantry. (Seriously, every single time.) I added a little extra chocolate flavor with cocoa powder and finished them off with chopped hazelnuts. The best part is that this is a quick cookie recipe—no dough chilling needed!

Prep time: 10 minutes • **Total time:** 45 minutes • **Makes:** 16 cookies

1 cup (125g) all-purpose flour

2 tsp unsweetened cocoa powder

½ tsp baking soda

½ tsp baking powder

½ tsp salt

2 cups (160g) old-fashioned oats

½ cup (115g) butter, melted

½ cup (100g) granulated sugar

½ cup (100g) light brown sugar

1 egg

1 tsp vanilla extract

½ cup (296g) Nutella®

¾ cup (85g) chopped hazelnuts

1. Whisk the flour, cocoa powder, baking soda, baking powder, salt, and oats together in a large bowl. Set aside.

2. In a medium bowl, whisk the melted butter, granulated sugar, brown sugar, egg, and vanilla extract together until completely combined. Whisk in the Nutella®. Pour the wet ingredients into the dry ingredients and mix together with a large spoon or rubber spatula until combined. Fold in the hazelnuts.

3. Preheat the oven to 350°F (175°C). Line two large cookie sheets with parchment paper or silicone baking mats.

4. Scoop the dough out of the bowl using a large cookie scoop or roll into balls (about 2 tablespoons of dough per cookie). Arrange the balls 3in (7.5cm) apart on the cookie sheet and slightly flatten each before baking. Flattening helps the cookies spread evenly as they bake.

5. Bake the cookies for 10–11 minutes, or until they are set on the sides. The cookies will look very soft in the centers. Allow to cool on the cookie sheets for 5 minutes before transferring to a wire rack to cool completely. The cookies will stay fresh in an airtight container at room temperature for up to 7 days.

TRIPLE CHOCOLATE BISCOTTI

Biscotti are one of those extra-special treats to enjoy with a good friend and a great cup of coffee. Baking biscotti at home may seem intimidating, but I assure you that there is nothing to fear. It's a simple dough that gets shaped into two slabs (how appetizing does that sound?) and baked twice. This homemade version is all about the chocolate because nothing goes better with coffee and friends.

Prep time: 40 minutes • **Total time:** 2 hours • **Makes:** 32 cookies

1¾ cups (220g) all-purpose flour (plus more for your hands)

½ cup (64g) unsweetened cocoa powder

1 cup (200g) granulated sugar

1 tsp baking soda

½ tsp salt

5 tbsp butter, cold and cubed

3 eggs

1 tsp espresso powder (optional, but recommended)

1 tsp vanilla extract

10oz (284g) coarsely chopped semi-sweet chocolate, such as Baker's brand, divided

¾ cup (88g) chopped walnuts

egg wash: 1 egg, beaten, with 1 tbsp milk

1 Preheat the oven to 350°F (175°C). Line two large cookie sheets with parchment paper or silicone baking mats. Set aside.

2. Whisk the flour, cocoa powder, granulated sugar, baking soda, and salt together in a large bowl. Using a pastry cutter or your hands, cut in the butter until the mixture is crumbly. Set aside.

3. In a medium bowl, whisk the eggs, espresso powder (if using), and vanilla extract together. Pour into the flour/butter mixture, and then gently mix with a large spoon or rubber spatula until everything is just barely moistened. Fold in 4 ounces (113g) of chopped chocolate and the walnuts.

4. Turn dough out onto a lightly floured surface, and with floured hands, knead lightly until the dough is soft and slightly sticky, about 8–10 times. If it's very sticky, knead 1–2 more tablespoon(s) of flour into the dough. With floured hands, divide the dough in two and place each half onto a cookie sheet. Shape each half into a 9-in-long (23cm) by 5-in-wide (13cm) slab, patting down until each is about ½in (12mm) thick. Using a pastry brush, lightly brush the top and sides of each slab with egg wash.

5. Bake slabs for 20–21 minutes. Remove from the oven but do not turn off the heat. Allow slabs to cool for 10 minutes. Once the slabs are cool enough to handle, cut each into 1-in-thick (2.5cm) slices.

6. Set slices cut sides up, ¼in (6mm) apart, on the baking sheets. Return to the oven to continue baking for about 8–9 minutes. Turn biscotti over and bake on other sides for 6–7 minutes. The cookies will be slightly soft in the centers with harder edges. Remove from the oven and allow to cool for 5 minutes on the cookie sheet. Transfer biscotti to a wire rack set to cool completely. As the biscotti cools, it becomes crunchy.

7. Melt the remaining chopped chocolate in a small microwave-safe bowl in 20-second increments until melted, stirring well after each increment. (Or you can use a double boiler; see *Sally Says* on page 87.) Drizzle biscotti with chocolate.

8. Allow chocolate to set in the refrigerator or at room temperature, about 30 minutes, before enjoying. Biscotti will stay fresh in an airtight container for up to 10 days.

LEMON SLICE 'N BAKE COOKIES

I've always enjoyed making slice 'n bake cookies because they're so simple, but their flavor has always been lacking. So I took what I love about sugar cookies and shortbread cookies, combined them, and created these. I love to add a little lemon flavor to the cookie dough and finishing them off with the lemon glaze is a necessity. The wonderful part is that you can slice off a few cookies at a time when the craving hits. Most of the magic happens in the refrigerator, so don't skip chilling the logs of dough.

Prep time: 4 hours, 25 minutes • **Total time:** 5 hours • **Makes:** 18–20 cookies

Cookies

¾ cup (170g) butter, softened to room temperature

⅔ cup (135g) granulated sugar

1 egg

1 tsp vanilla extract

1 tsp lemon extract

1 tbsp lemon zest

2 cups (250g) all-purpose flour (plus more for your hands)

¼ tsp salt

½ cup (96g) coarse sugar or yellow sparkling sugar for rolling (I use Wilton brand)

Lemon Glaze

1¼ cups (150g) confectioners' sugar

3 tbsp fresh lemon juice, divided

½ tsp vanilla extract

1. **MAKE THE COOKIES:** Using a hand-held or stand mixer fitted with a paddle attachment, beat the butter in a large bowl on high speed for 1 minute. Once creamy and smooth, add the granulated sugar. Beat on medium speed until fluffy and light in color. Beat in the egg, vanilla extract, lemon extract, and lemon zest on high speed until combined. Scrape down the sides of the bowl as needed. Add the flour and salt. Beat everything together on low speed for 1 minute, or until combined. The cookie dough will be thick and slightly sticky.

2. Turn the dough out onto a floured work surface, and with floured hands, divide into two. Shape each half into an 8-in-long (20cm) log, about 2½in (6.25cm) in diameter. Tightly wrap the logs in plastic wrap and chill in the refrigerator for at least 4 hours and up to 5 days. Chilling is important for this cookie dough. I prefer to chill the logs overnight.

3. Preheat the oven to 350°F (175°C). Line two large cookie sheets with parchment paper or silicone baking mats. Set aside. Pour coarse sugar onto a large plate.

4. Remove logs from the refrigerator and roll into coarse sugar. Slice each log into 9 or 10 equally thick cookies and place cookies on the cookie sheets about 2in (5cm) apart.

5. Bake the cookies for 12–14 minutes, or until brown around the edges. Allow to cool on the cookie sheets for 5 minutes before transferring to a wire rack to cool completely before glazing.

6. **MAKE THE GLAZE:** Whisk the confectioners' sugar, 2 tablespoons of lemon juice, and vanilla extract together. It will be very thick. Whisk in 1 (or more) tablespoon(s) of juice, depending on how thick you'd like the glaze. Drizzle glaze over completely cooled cookies. Cookies will stay fresh in an airtight container at room temperature for up to 2 days or in the refrigerator for up to 7.

CHOCOLATE CHIP COOKIE BITES

These cookie bites are almost too cute to eat, but that won't stop you from inhaling about ten at a time. They're mini so calories don't count . . . right?

Prep time: 25 minutes • **Total time:** 35 minutes • **Makes:** 85 bite-sized cookies

1⅔ cups (210g) all-purpose flour

½ tsp baking soda

¼ tsp salt

½ cup (115g) butter, softened to room temperature

½ cup (100g) light brown sugar

½ cup (100g) granulated sugar

1 egg

1 tsp vanilla extract

¾ cup (135g) mini chocolate chips

1. Preheat the oven to 350°F (175°F). Line two large cookie sheets with parchment paper or silicone baking mats.

2. Whisk the flour, baking soda, and salt together in a medium bowl. Set aside.

3. Using a hand-held or stand mixer fitted with a paddle attachment, beat the butter in a large bowl on high speed for 1 minute. Once creamy and smooth, add the brown sugar and granulated sugar. Beat on medium speed until fluffy and light in color. Beat in the egg and vanilla extract, scraping down the sides of the bowl as needed.

4. Slowly add the dry ingredients to the wet ingredients with the mixer running on low speed. Continue to beat until everything is combined. Using a large spoon or rubber spatula, fold in the mini chocolate chips.

5. Roll the dough into tiny balls, about 1 teaspoon of dough each. Place on the cookie sheet about 1in (2.5cm) apart.

6. Bake for 7–8 minutes, or until the edges are lightly browned. Slightly flatten each cookie with the back of a spoon if they did not spread much. Allow to cool on the cookie sheets for 5 minutes before transferring to a wire rack to cool completely. The cookies will stay fresh in an airtight container at room temperature for up to 7 days.

 SALLY SAYS: If you're going for ultra-cuteness, press a couple of mini chocolate chips into the tops of the cookies right after they come out of the oven.

COCONUT LIME COOKIES

I wish I could tell you that I dreamed up these cookies on a tropical beach somewhere, but the reality is I made them on the coldest, rainiest, grayest day of the month—which actually worked in my favor because it felt like paradise inside my kitchen! There's so much to love in these cookies: the zippy lime flavor, the coconut packed inside, the chewy edges, and the silky-smooth lime glaze. Not quite coastal living, but pretty darn close!

Prep time: 25 minutes • **Total time:** 2 hours, 40 minutes • **Makes:** 32–36 cookies

Cookies

3 cups (375g) all-purpose flour

1 tsp baking soda

½ tsp baking powder

½ tsp salt

1 cup (230g) butter, softened to room temperature

1½ cups (300g) granulated sugar

2 eggs

1 tsp vanilla extract

1 tsp coconut extract

1 tbsp lime juice

1 tbsp lime zest

1 cup (73g) flaked/shredded coconut (sweetened), divided

Lime Glaze

1¼ cups (150g) confectioners' sugar

3 tbsp fresh lime juice, divided

½ tsp vanilla extract

1. **MAKE THE COOKIES:** Whisk the flour, baking soda, baking powder, and salt together in a large bowl. Set aside.

2. Using a hand-held or stand mixer fitted with a paddle attachment, beat the butter in a separate large bowl on high speed for 1 minute. Once creamy and smooth, add the granulated sugar. Beat on medium speed until fluffy and light in color. Beat in the eggs, vanilla extract, coconut extract, lime juice, and lime zest until combined. Scrape down the sides of the bowl as needed.

3. Slowly add the dry ingredients to the wet ingredients with the mixer running on low speed. Continue to beat until everything is combined. Using a large spoon or rubber spatula, fold in ⅔ cup coconut. Cover the dough and chill for at least 2 hours or up to 3 days.

4. Take the dough out of the refrigerator and allow to soften slightly at room temperature for 10 minutes.

5. Preheat the oven to 350°F (175°C). Line two large cookie sheets with parchment paper or silicone baking mats.

6. Roll the dough into balls, about 1 heaping tablespoon of dough per cookie. Place on the cookie sheet about 3in (7.5cm) apart.

7. Bake for 9–11 minutes, or until the edges are lightly browned. Remove from the oven but do not turn off the heat. Allow cookies to cool on the cookie sheets for 5 minutes before transferring to a wire rack to cool completely. Lower oven temperature to 300°F (150°C). Spread the remaining coconut onto a cookie sheet lined with parchment paper or silicone baking mat. Bake for 6–8 minutes, or until coconut is lightly browned. Allow coconut cool on the pan for 10 minutes before sprinkling on top of cookies.

8. **MAKE THE GLAZE:** Whisk the confectioners' sugar, 2 tablespoons of lime juice, and vanilla extract together. It will be very thick. Whisk in 1 (or more) tablespoon(s) of juice, depending on how thick you'd like the glaze. Drizzle glaze over completely cooled cookies and top with toasted coconut. Cookies will stay fresh in an airtight container at room temperature for up to 2 days or in the refrigerator for up to 7.

CHOCOLATE WHOOPIE PIES

These classic cookie sandwiches win the hearts of anyone who takes that first satisfying bite. They're basically cake-like chocolate cookies with a super creamy and sweet marshmallow filling . . . and, yes, they're completely irresistible. So fun to eat and fun to say! Try individually wrapping each whoopie pie in plastic for bake sales or for gifting to friends.

Prep time: 30 minutes • **Total time:** 1 hour • **Makes:** 9 whoopie pies

COOKIES

- 2 cups (250g) all-purpose flour
- 6 tbsp unsweetened cocoa powder
- 1¼ tsp baking soda
- ½ tsp salt
- ½ cup (115g) butter, softened to room temperature
- 1 cup (200g) light brown sugar
- 1 egg
- 1½ tsp vanilla extract
- 1 cup (240ml) buttermilk divided

FILLING

- ½ cup (115g) butter, softened to room temperature
- 1½ cups (180g) confectioners' sugar
- 1 tsp vanilla extract
- 2 cups (384g) marshmallow crème (such as Fluff®)

1. **MAKE THE COOKIES:** Preheat the oven to 350°F (175°C). Line two large cookie sheets with parchment paper or silicone baking mats.

2. Whisk the flour, cocoa powder, baking soda, and salt together in a large bowl. Set aside.

3. Using a hand-held or stand mixer fitted with a paddle attachment, beat the butter in a large bowl on high speed for 1 minute. Once creamy and smooth, add the brown sugar. Beat on high speed for 2 full minutes, then beat in the egg and vanilla extract until combined. Scrape down the sides of the bowl as needed.

4. With the mixer running on low speed, add one-third of the dry ingredients to the wet ingredients. Then, add half the buttermilk. Repeat with the remaining dry ingredients and buttermilk until everything is smooth and combined. The dough will resemble a thick cake batter.

5. Spoon mounds, 3 tablespoons each, onto the cookie sheets about 3in (7.5cm) apart.

6. Bake the cookies for 10–12 minutes, or until the tops spring back when touched. Allow to cool on the cookie sheets for 5 minutes before transferring to a wire rack to cool completely before sandwiching.

7. **MAKE THE FILLING:** Using a hand-held or stand mixer fitted with a whisk attachment, beat the butter in a large bowl on high speed for 1 minute. Once creamy and smooth, beat in the confectioners' sugar and vanilla extract on low speed, gradually increasing to high speed as the mixture combines. Finally, beat in the marshmallow crème on medium-high speed until smooth and combined.

8. Pair the cookies based on their size. Spread marshmallow filling on the flat side of half of the cookies, then sandwich the cookies together. Cookies will stay fresh in an airtight container at room temperature for up to 2 days or in the refrigerator for up to 7.

 SALLY SAYS: My number one tip? Use a cookie scoop. I use the large size, which holds a scant 3 tablespoons of dough per cookie. A cookie scoop keeps the sizes uniform so they sandwich together nicely.

CUPCAKES

What is it about cupcakes that is so appealing? When I began to write this book, I asked blog readers to tell me why they love cupcakes so much. Decadent, flavorful, pretty, unique, and satisfying were all words that came to mind. The following eight recipes fit the mold for each spot-on description from my cupcake focus group.

Cupcakes are simply small cakes, which makes them the perfect size for a single serving. They're easy to share, easy to eat, and there are no extra plates or forks to wash at the end of the day. Their tiny charm is simply irresistible.

Making the following cupcakes requires no special training. Mix and match the frostings and cupcakes, decorate them how you please, and make each batch truly your own. Salted Caramel Whipped Cream (page 148) tastes divine on Carrot Cake Cupcakes (page 144), and Strawberry Whipped Cream (page 70) on Sunshine Lemon Cupcakes (page 143) makes one cool summery treat. Or you can just make the delicious White Chocolate Raspberry Cupcakes (page 140 and the opposite page) exactly as they are!

When it comes to cupcakes, it's okay to break the rules!

WHITE CHOCOLATE RASPBERRY CUPCAKES

A basic vanilla cupcake recipe can take you far in life. Once you master the recipe, the doors to creative cupcake land are wide open. I took my favorite basic vanilla cupcake recipe (page 155), filled them with raspberry, and topped them off with a generous swirl of white chocolate. This frosting is legendary! It's a perfectly thick, creamy, and smooth white chocolate frosting. Each bite of these cupcakes will fill your mouth with juicy raspberry, fluffy vanilla cake, and an explosion of white chocolate. With a plethora of tastes and textures, I crown these cupcakes as one of the best.

Prep time: 20 minutes • **Total time:** 40 minutes, plus cooling • **Makes:** 12 cupcakes

Cupcakes

1⅔ cups (210g) all-purpose flour

½ tsp baking powder

¼ tsp baking soda

½ tsp salt

½ cup (115g) butter, melted

1 cup (200g) granulated sugar

1 egg

¼ cup (60g) Greek or regular yogurt (plain or vanilla)

¾ cup (180ml) milk

2 tsp vanilla extract

¼ cup (80g) raspberry jam

White Chocolate Frosting

1 cup (230g) butter, softened to room temperature

2 cups (240g) confectioners' sugar

6oz (170g) white chocolate, melted and slightly cooled

¼ cup (60ml) heavy cream

1 tsp vanilla extract

¼ tsp salt

12 raspberries (optional)

1 Preheat the oven to 350°F (175°C) Line 12-count muffin pan with cupcake liners. Set aside.

2 **MAKE THE CUPCAKES:** Whisk the flour, baking powder, baking soda, and salt together in a large bowl. Set aside. In a large microwave-safe bowl, melt the butter in the microwave. Add the granulated sugar and whisk vigorously until no sugar lumps remain—the mixture will be gritty. Whisk in the egg, yogurt, milk, and vanilla until combined. Slowly whisk the wet ingredients into the dry ingredients until no lumps remain. Do not overmix the batter.

3 Pour the batter evenly into the 12 cupcake liners. Bake for 20 minutes, rotating the pan halfway through baking, or until a toothpick inserted in the center comes out clean. Remove from the oven and allow to cool completely before filling and frosting. While the cupcakes are cooling, melt the white chocolate for the frosting in a double boiler or in 20-second increments in the microwave, stirring after each increment. Allow to slightly cool.

4 **FILL THE CUPCAKES:** Using a sharp knife, cut a circular hole into the center of the cooled cupcake to create a little pocket about ½ in (13mm) deep. Do not discard the core of cake you removed. Place 1 teaspoon of raspberry jam inside and top with the piece of cupcake you removed to seal. Repeat with all 12 cupcakes.

5 **MAKE THE FROSTING:** In a medium bowl using a handheld or stand mixer fitted with a paddle attachment, beat the butter on medium speed for 1 minute. Switch the mixer to low speed and slowly add the confectioners' sugar. Quickly stir the cooled white chocolate so that it is smooth and add to the butter/sugar mixture. Switch the mixer to medium speed and beat for 2 minutes until combined and creamy. Add the cream, vanilla extract, and salt. Beat for 1 minute until combined. The frosting will be ready to use immediately, so you can frost the cupcakes (I used a Wilton 1M swirl tip) and top with a raspberry. The cupcakes will stay fresh stored in the refrigerator for up to 3 days.

SALLY SAYS:
This is my favorite
way to fill cupcakes.
It's so easy! Simply
cut a hole in the center
of the cupcake to
create a little pocket.
Sometimes I like to fill
them with strawberry
jam or even Nutella®.
Seal it in with the
piece of cupcake you
removed. Want to see
what these cupcakes
look like when they're
frosted and finished?
Check out page 138.

SUNSHINE LEMON CUPCAKES

When life throws you lemons, make a dozen cupcakes! This is one of my favorite cupcake recipes. Readers may think I'm a chocoholic, but I love the fresh flavor of lemon in my desserts. There is just something irresistible about a soft, fluffy lemon cupcake and a tart cream cheese icing. Be sure to use fresh lemon juice on this recipe for the best flavor.

Prep time: 20 minutes • **Total time:** 40 minutes, plus cooling • **Makes:** 12 cupcakes

CUPCAKES

½ cup (115g) butter, softened to room temperature

1 cup (or 200g) granulated sugar

2 eggs

2 tsp vanilla extract

1½ cups (190g) all-purpose flour

2 tsp baking powder

½ tsp salt

½ cup (120ml) milk

zest and juice of 2 medium lemons

LEMON CREAM CHEESE FROSTING

8oz (224g) full-fat cream cheese, softened to room temperature

¼ cup (60g) butter, softened to room temperature

zest and juice of 1 medium lemon, plus extra zest to decorate (optional)

2 cups (240g) confectioners' sugar

1   Preheat the oven to 350°F (175°C). Line a 12-count muffin pan with cupcake liners. Set aside.

2   **MAKE THE CUPCAKES:** In a large bowl using a handheld or stand mixer fitted with a paddle attachment, beat the butter and granulated sugar together on medium speed until creamed, about 2–3 minutes. Add the eggs and vanilla and beat on medium speed until everything is combined and pale in color, about 2 full minutes. Set aside.

3   Whisk the flour, baking powder, and salt together in a medium bowl. Slowly add the dry ingredients to the wet ingredients in 3 additions, stirring with a large rubber spatula or spoon after each addition—the batter will be thick. Add the milk, lemon zest, and lemon juice. Mix until just combined, do not overmix.

4   Pour the batter evenly into 12 cupcake liners. Bake for about 18–20 minutes, rotating the pan halfway through baking. A toothpick inserted in the middle will come out clean when done. Remove from the oven and allow to cool completely before frosting.

5   **MAKE THE FROSTING:** In a medium bowl using a handheld or stand mixer fitted with a paddle attachment, beat the cream cheese and butter together on medium speed until smooth, about 2 minutes. Add the lemon juice and lemon zest. Continue to beat for 1 minute. Switch the mixer to low speed and slowly add the confectioners' sugar. Switch to medium speed and beat for 2 minutes until combined and creamy. Frost the cupcakes and top with additional lemon zest if desired. I used a Wilton #12 piping tip. Serve the cupcakes chilled. The cupcakes will remain fresh stored in the refrigerator for up to 4 days.

 SALLY SAYS: Buy a zester! I held off from buying a zester for years, but I am so glad I finally purchased my Microplane® zester. It was under $10 and worth every single penny. I use it to make these cupcakes, Glazed Lemon Loaf (page 5), Lemon Poppy-Seed Muffins (page 13), Chocolate Glazed Orange Macaroons (page 121), and Key Lime Pie (page 77).

CARROT CAKE CUPCAKES

My dad gave me blue eyes, blonde hair, and an unconditional love for carrot cake. We love this classic dessert so much that we simply call it birthday cake. My tried-and-true carrot cake recipe is one of the most popular recipes on my website. For good reasons too: it's super moist, super flavorful, and super easy to make. Since I can never seem to stop at one slice, I decided to turn my cake into individual cupcakes. They're finished off with a sweet, tangy cream cheese frosting that makes them a true crowd-pleaser.

Prep time: 20 minutes • **Total time:** 40 minutes, plus cooling • **Makes:** 14 cupcakes

Cupcakes

1 cup (200g) dark brown sugar

¾ cup (180ml) vegetable oil (or melted coconut oil)

¼ cup (60g) yogurt (Greek or regular yogurt, plain or vanilla)

3 eggs

2 tsp vanilla extract

2 cups (250g) all-purpose flour

1 tsp baking soda

2 tsp ground cinnamon

¼ tsp ground nutmeg

½ tsp salt

2 cups (260g) finely grated baby carrots (or regular carrots)

Cream Cheese Frosting

8oz (224g) full-fat cream cheese, softened to room temperature

¼ cup (60g) butter, softened to room temperature

1½ cups (190g) confectioners' sugar

1 tbsp milk

1 tsp vanilla extract

pinch salt

chopped pecans and orange chocolate candies, optional

1 Preheat the oven to 350°F (175°C). Line two 12-count muffin pans with 14 cupcake liners. Fill the unused cups one-third full with water to prevent warping. Set aside.

2 **MAKE THE CUPCAKES:** Whisk the brown sugar and oil together in a large bowl until combined. Whisk in the yogurt until fully incorporated and no lumps remain—the mixture will be thick. Add the eggs, one at a time, whisking well after each addition. Whisk in the vanilla. Set aside.

3 In a separate medium bowl, combine the flour, baking soda, cinnamon, nutmeg, and salt. With a rubber spatula or large spoon, stir the dry ingredients into the wet ingredients until just combined. Do not overmix. Fold in the finely grated carrots. Spoon the batter evenly into 14 cupcake liners. Bake for 16–18 minutes, rotating the pan halfway through baking, or until a toothpick inserted in the middle of a cupcake comes out clean. Allow to cool completely before frosting.

4 **MAKE THE FROSTING:** In a medium bowl using a handheld or stand mixer fitted with a paddle attachment, beat the cream cheese and butter together on medium speed until smooth, about 2 minutes. Add the confectioners' sugar and milk. Beat for 2 minutes. Add the vanilla and salt. Beat for 1 minute. For thicker frosting, add more confectioners' sugar and add extra salt to offset the additional sugar. Frost the cupcakes with a knife. Serve the cupcakes chilled. The cupcakes will remain fresh stored in the refrigerator for up to 4 days.

DARK CHOCOLATE BUTTERSCOTCH CUPCAKES

These are my "diet-buster" cupcakes. They're moist, fudgy, and completely dangerous for anyone watching their waistline. This thick and fluffy frosting takes a full bag of butterscotch morsels, butter, sugar, and cream. They're worth every calorie, trust me.

Prep time: 20 minutes • **Total time:** 40 minutes, plus cooling • **Makes:** 12 cupcakes

CUPCAKES

½ cup (115g) butter

2oz (112g) semi-sweet baking chocolate

½ cup (45g) unsweetened cocoa powder (not Dutch processed)

¾ cup (94g) all-purpose flour

½ tsp baking soda

¾ tsp baking powder

¼ tsp salt

2 eggs, at room temperature

½ cup (100g) granulated sugar

¼ cup (50g) light brown sugar

1 tsp vanilla extract

½ cup (120ml) buttermilk

BUTTERSCOTCH FROSTING

11-oz (312g) package butterscotch morsels, plus more for decorating (optional)

2–3 tsp vegetable shortening

1 cup (230g) butter, softened to room temperature

1¾ cups (210g) confectioners' sugar

2 tbsp heavy cream

pinch salt

1 Preheat the oven to 350°F (175°C). Line a 12-count muffin pan with cupcake liners. Set aside.

2 **MAKE THE CUPCAKES:** Melt the butter and chocolate together in the microwave or over a low heat on the stovetop. Stir until smooth and set aside to slightly cool.

3 Whisk the cocoa powder, flour, baking soda, baking powder, and salt together in a medium bowl. Set aside. In a large bowl, whisk the eggs, granulated sugar, and brown sugar together until smooth. Add the cooled butter/chocolate and whisk until smooth. Add half of the flour mixture, then half of the buttermilk. Stir. Repeat until everything is added. Stir until just combined, do not overmix. The batter will be very thick, like pudding.

4 Pour the batter evenly into 12 cupcake liners. Bake for 18 minutes, rotating the pan halfway through baking, or until a toothpick inserted in the center comes out clean. Remove from the oven and allow to cool completely before frosting.

5 **MAKE THE FROSTING:** Melt the butterscotch morsels and 2 teaspoons of shortening together in the microwave in 30-second increments, stirring vigorously until smooth. Add 1 more teaspoon of shortening if the mixture is too thick (See *Sally Says*, below). Allow to cool. In a medium bowl using a handheld or stand mixer fitted with a paddle attachment, beat the butter on medium speed for 1 minute. Switch the mixer to low speed and slowly add the confectioners' sugar. Quickly stir the cooled butterscotch/shortening so that it is smooth and add to the butter/sugar mixture. Switch the mixer to medium speed and beat for 2 minutes until combined. Add the cream and salt. Beat for 2 minutes until creamy.

6 Frost the cupcakes and sprinkle with additional butterscotch chips if desired. I used a Wilton #12 piping tip. The cupcakes will stay fresh stored at room temperature for up to 3 days.

 SALLY SAYS: Butterscotch morsels will not melt properly without shortening. Microwave them together in short increments, stirring after each time until smooth. As the mixture cools, it will turn solid, but don't worry. Twenty seconds in the microwave will help smooth the mixture for inclusion in the frosting.

APPLE SPICE CUPCAKES with SALTED CARAMEL WHIPPED CREAM

When the weather starts to get cooler and I sadly kiss those long summer days goodbye, I make a batch of these spice cupcakes and all is right in the world again. Buttery and moist, these flavorful cupcakes are full of tart apples, cinnamon, nutmeg, and sweet brown sugar. In fact, the cupcakes pack enough flavor that you don't even need a topping! But there's always room for a little whipped cream. Especially one infused with salted caramel …

Prep time: 15 minutes • **Total time:** 40 minutes, plus cooling • **Makes:** 12 cupcakes

Cupcakes

½ cup (115g) butter, melted

⅓ cup (65g) granulated sugar

⅔ cup (135g) dark brown sugar

2 eggs

⅓ cup (80ml) milk

2 tsp vanilla extract

1½ cups (190g) all-purpose flour

¼ tsp baking powder

1 tsp baking soda

½ tsp salt

1 tsp ground cinnamon

½ tsp ground nutmeg

1 large Granny Smith apple, peeled and finely chopped

Caramel Whipped Cream

1½ cups (300ml) heavy cream

¼ cup (80g) room temperature salted caramel sauce (page 91)

1 tbsp dark brown sugar

1   Preheat the oven to 350°F (175°C). Line a 12-count muffin pan with cupcake liners. Set aside.

2   **MAKE THE CUPCAKES:** Whisk the melted butter, granulated sugar, and brown sugar together in a medium bowl until combined. Whisk in the eggs, one at a time, until smooth. Add the milk and vanilla, whisking until combined. Set aside.

3   Whisk the flour, baking powder, baking soda, salt, cinnamon, and nutmeg together in a large bowl. Slowly add the wet ingredients to the dry ingredients and stir gently until combined. The batter will have a few lumps. Fold in the apple.

4   Fill the cupcake liners ¾ of the way full with batter. Bake for 21–23 minutes, rotating the pan halfway through baking. A toothpick inserted in the center will come out clean when done. Remove from the oven and allow to cool completely before frosting.

5   **MAKE THE WHIPPED CREAM:** Using a hand-held or stand mixer fitted with a whisk attachment, whip the cream, salted caramel, and brown sugar together in a medium bowl on high speed until stiff peaks begin to form, about 4–5 full minutes. Frost the cupcakes with a knife. Drizzle with additional salted caramel sauce if desired. Serve the cupcakes chilled. The cupcakes will remain fresh stored in the refrigerator for up to 4 days.

MINT CHOCOLATE CHIP ICE CREAM CUPCAKES

There is nothing quite like a giant waffle cone filled with mint chocolate chip ice cream on a hot sunny day. That is, however, until I made these crowd-pleaser cupcakes. Each creamy mint chocolate bite sits atop an easy Oreo® cookie crust. I like to finish them off with a thick chocolate drizzle and a generous dollop of whipped cream. Move that frozen lasagna and bag of veggies to the side to make room for your new favorite frozen treat!

Prep time: 15 minutes • **Total time:** 4 hours, 15 minutes • **Makes:** 12 cupcakes

CRUST

10 Oreo® cookies, crushed into crumbs

2 tbsp butter, melted

FILLING

8oz (226g) container frozen whipped topping, thawed

1qt (950ml) mint chocolate chip ice cream, softened

TOPPING

4oz (225g) coarsely chopped semi-sweet chocolate, such as Baker's brand

¾ cup (30g) whipped cream

1 Line a 12-count muffin pan with cupcake liners. Set aside.

2 **MAKE THE CRUST:** Combine the crushed Oreos® and melted butter in a medium bowl. Divide between 12 cupcake liners and press evenly into the bottom of each. Set aside.

3 **MAKE THE FILLING:** In a large bowl, stir the frozen whipped topping and ice cream together until softened and combined evenly. Spoon the mixture evenly into the prepared liners. Freeze for at least 4 hours or until firm.

4 **MAKE THE TOPPING:** Right before removing cupcakes from the freezer, melt the semi-sweet chocolate in a small bowl in the microwave in 20-second increments, stirring after each increment until smooth. Remove the cupcakes from the freezer and drizzle melted chocolate over each. Top each cupcake with 1 tablespoon of whipped cream.

5 The chocolate-drizzled cupcakes may be made 1 day in advance and garnished with whipped cream immediately before serving.

NUTELLA®-FROSTED BANANA CUPCAKES

Nutella® frosting has to be one of the best uses of this chocolate hazelnut spread. I make this frosting often because it tastes divine paired with just about anything. It's light, fluffy, and reminiscent of creamy chocolate mousse. To make the super-moist banana cupcakes, simply use the Banana Chocolate Chip Layer Cake recipe (page 69), excluding the chocolate chips (or not!) and pour into cupcake liners. Keep a bunch of ripe bananas in your freezer and thaw when ready to use. Trust me, you'll always want to be prepared to make a batch of these.

Prep time: 20 minutes • **Total time:** 40 minutes, plus cooling • **Makes:** 18 cupcakes

CUPCAKES

Batter for Banana Chocolate Chip Layer Cake, with or without chocolate chips (page 69)

NUTELLA® FROSTING

1 cup (230g) butter, softened to room temperature

2 cups (240g) confectioners' sugar

¾ cup (225g) Nutella®

3 tbsp heavy cream

2 tsp vanilla extract

pinch salt

banana chips for decoration (optional)

1   Preheat the oven to 350°F (175°C). Line two 12-count muffin pans with 18 cupcake liners. Set aside.

2   **MAKE THE CUPCAKES:** Prepare the batter for banana chocolate chip layer cake, with or without chocolate chips. Pour evenly into 18 cupcake liners. Fill the unused cups one-third full with water to prevent warping. Bake each batch for 17–19 minutes, rotating the pan halfway through baking, or until a toothpick inserted in the middle of a cupcake comes out clean. Allow to cool completely before frosting.

3   **MAKE THE FROSTING.** In a medium bowl using a handheld or stand mixer fitted with a paddle attachment, beat the butter on medium speed for 1 minute. Switch the mixer to low speed and slowly add the confectioners' sugar and Nutella®. Switch to medium speed and beat for 2 minutes until combined and creamy. Add the heavy cream, vanilla extract and salt and beat for 1 minute. If the frosting is too thick, add more heavy cream (1 tablespoon measurements at a time). If the frosting is too thin, add more confectioners' sugar (¼ cup or 30g at a time).

4   Frost the cooled cupcakes and garnish with banana chips, if desired. I used a Wilton #12 tip to pipe the frosting. The cupcakes will stay fresh stored in the refrigerator for up to 3 days.

MINI VANILLA BEAN CUPCAKES

Every time I make these mini cupcakes, I am eight years old all over again. The bite-sized treats are completely irresistible with their fluffy texture and smooth buttery taste. I cap them with a tall kiss of vanilla bean frosting and finish them off with a shower of colorful sprinkles. These nostalgic little cupcakes put any other birthday dessert to shame!

Prep time: 15 minutes • **Total time:** 30 minutes, plus cooling • **Makes:** 32–36 mini cupcakes

CUPCAKES

1⅔ cups (210g) all-purpose flour

½ tsp baking powder

¼ tsp baking soda

½ tsp salt

½ cup (115g) butter, melted

1 cup (200g) granulated sugar

1 egg

¼ cup (60ml) yogurt (plain or vanilla; Greek or regular)

¾ cup (180ml) milk

2 tsp vanilla extract

VANILLA BEAN FROSTING

¾ cup (170g) butter, softened to room temperature

3–4 cups (360–480g) confectioners' sugar

3 tbsp heavy cream

1 tsp vanilla extract

seeds scraped from ½ vanilla bean (See *Sally Says*, right)

pinch salt

rainbow sprinkles

1   Preheat the oven to 350°F (175°C). Line 24-count mini-muffin pan with cupcake liners or spray with non-stick spray. Set aside.

2   **MAKE THE CUPCAKES.** Whisk the flour, baking powder, baking soda, and salt together in a large bowl. Set aside. In a large microwave-safe bowl, melt the butter in the microwave. Whisk in the sugar, egg, yogurt, milk, and vanilla until combined. Slowly whisk the wet ingredients into the dry ingredients until no lumps remain. Do not overmix the batter.

3   Fill the cupcake liners ¾ of the way full with batter. Bake for 11–12 minutes or until a toothpick inserted in the center comes out clean. Remove from oven and allow to cool completely before frosting.

4   **MAKE THE FROSTING.** In a medium bowl using a handheld or stand mixer fitted with a paddle attachment, beat the butter on medium speed for 1 minute. Add the confectioners' sugar and beat for 1 minute. Add the heavy cream, vanilla, vanilla seeds, and salt. Beat on high for 2 minutes until thick and creamy. Add more confectioners' sugar if the frosting is too thin; add more heavy cream if the frosting is too thick. Frost the cupcakes and top with sprinkles. I used a Wilton #12 tip to pipe the frosting. The cupcakes will stay fresh stored in the refrigerator for up to 3 days.

 SALLY SAYS: I love adding seeds from half of a split vanilla bean to the frosting. The vanilla bean is completely optional, but I highly recommend it for the best flavor. Feel free to add the rest of the seeds from the split vanilla bean to the cupcake batter when you're mixing in the vanilla extract.

HEALTHIER CHOICES

While I was certainly born with a sweet tooth, I find it doubly satisfying to indulge in lighter fare that I can actually feeling good about eating. As a baker, I am around tempting desserts and pastries every single day. My counter is a smorgasbord of brownies, cookies, breads, and cupcakes galore. I taste-test it all and the leftovers go off to friends, family, neighbors, and donations. If only we lived in a world where I could eat it all and still fit into my skinny jeans!

Healthier treats such as granola (page 166), apple chips (page 175), and whole-grain muffins (page 165) are what I enjoy in my daily diet. It's easy to incorporate nutritious ingredients like whole grains and fruits into your baked (and not-baked) goodies without sacrificing taste or texture. Who says chocolate cake (page 170) should be off limits? Certainly not me.

I created the following chapter with food allergies and preferences in mind. You'll find the recipes marked as gluten free and/or vegan if applicable. It's important to note that several recipes are naturally gluten-free and vegan, but you should always use "certified" gluten-free ingredients (like oats) or non-dairy milk (for vegans), so be sure and check your labels before you begin baking. I also give a few suggestions for ways to adapt the recipes to fit either category. No matter what your diet is, no one should miss out on dessert!

BLUEBERRY ALMOND OAT SQUARES

Blueberries are a nutritional powerhouse and one of my favorite fruits to bake with. See pages 14 and 35 for proof! These easy squares are healthy enough to call breakfast. They're made with whole wheat flour, oats, almonds, and sweetened with maple syrup. The thick oatmeal base is hearty and there's enough blueberry filling to make pancakes jealous (page 35). I like to add a tart Granny Smith apple to offset the sweet blueberry filling.

Prep time: 15 minutes • **Total time:** 45 minutes, plus cooling • **Makes:** 16 squares

Blueberry Filling

2 tbsp cornstarch

2 tbsp warm water

2 cups (345g) fresh blueberries (or frozen and unthawed)

¼ cup (80g) pure maple syrup

1 tbsp granulated sugar

1 Granny Smith apple, peeled and thinly sliced

Oatmeal Crust & Topping

2 cups (160g) old-fashioned oats

⅓ cup (45g) whole wheat flour

1 tsp ground cinnamon

1 cup (250g) almond butter

¼ cup (80g) pure maple syrup

¼ cup (55g) apple butter

1 egg, beaten

½ cup (50g) sliced almonds

1   **MAKE THE BLUEBERRY FILLING:** Mix the cornstarch with the warm water until all of the cornstarch has dissolved and there are no more clumps. It should resemble milk. Set aside. Combine the blueberries, maple syrup, and sugar together in a small saucepan over medium heat. Bring to a boil and stir well. Smash some of the blueberries down as you stir. Remove from the heat and stir in the pre-mixed cornstarch. Whisk until all the clumps are gone and set aside to thicken and cool.

2   Preheat the oven to 325°F (160°C). Line an 8 x 8-in (20 x 20cm) baking pan with aluminum foil with enough overhang on the sides for easy removal. Set aside.

3   **MAKE THE OAT CRUST/TOPPING:** Combine the oats, whole wheat flour, cinnamon, almond butter, maple syrup, apple butter, and beaten egg in a large bowl. Mix until all of the oats are moistened and the mixture is thoroughly combined—the mixture will be sticky. Reserve ½ cup (80g) and press the remaining oat mixture into the prepared baking pan. Make sure it is firmly pressed down.

4   Spread the blueberry filling on top. Evenly layer the sliced apples on top of the blueberry filling. To the reserved oat mixture, add the sliced almonds. Crumble this over the filling and, using the back of a spatula, press the topping down firmly into the filling. You want to make sure it sticks well.

5   Bake for 25–30 minutes—the topping will be lightly browned. Allow to cool for 30 minutes at room temperature. Transfer to the refrigerator and chill for 2 hours. Lift the foil out of the pan using the overhang on the sides and cut into squares. These squares will remain fresh stored in an airtight container in the refrigerator for up to 5 days. Bars can be frozen up to 2 months.

APPLE CINNAMON RAISIN BREAKFAST COOKIES

I love cookies so much that I eat them for breakfast. When I'm in workout mode and have the itch to fuel my body with some clean eats, I make a batch of these cinnamon-spiced cookies. They're stuffed with a bunch of my favorite superfoods like oats, bananas, and apples. Some bonus points? They're whole grain, all-natural, dairy-free, gluten-free and yes, they actually taste good! All you need is one bowl and 25 minutes. Healthy breakfast is served.

Prep time: 10 minutes • **Total time:** 25 minutes • **Makes:** 10 large cookies

2 cups (160g) quick-cooking oats (not whole oats)

¾ tsp salt

2 tsp ground cinnamon

¾ cup (185g) peanut butter

¼ cup (80g) pure maple syrup

⅓ cup (70g) apple butter

1 large banana, mashed (about ½ cup or 115g)

1 cup (85g) dried apples, diced

½ cup (70g) raisins

1 Preheat the oven to 325°F (160°C). Line a large cookie sheet with parchment paper or a silicone baking mat. Set aside.

2 Combine all of the ingredients into a large bowl and mix by hand with a rubber spatula. Mix until all of the ingredients are combined. The dough will be quite stiff.

3 Take ¼ cup (35g) of dough, drop it onto the prepared cookie sheet and slightly flatten the top into the desired thickness. The cookies will not spread in the oven. Repeat with the remaining dough.

4 Bake for 15–16 minutes, or until the edges are slightly brown. Allow to cool completely on the cookie sheets. The cookies will remain fresh in an airtight container at room temperature or in the refrigerator for 1 week. Cookies can be frozen up to 3 months.

 SALLY SAYS: Double this recipe and freeze your leftover cookies for a quick grab and go breakfast or snack. My freezer is stocked with them! Instead of raisins and apples, fill them your other favorites like nuts, chocolate chips, pumpkin seeds, and coconut.

 VEGAN & GLUTEN-FREE

PUMPKIN GRANOLA BARS

The first time I ever made these chewy granola bars was the day I locked my keys in the car. Luckily, I had a couple of these stashed away in my purse as I awaited AAA to come save the day. Biting into one as I stared at my watch made even the most inconvenient situation enjoyable. Each cinnamon-spiced bite is packed with nutrient-rich powerhouses like whole grain oats, pumpkin purée, and pumpkin seeds. The chocolate chips are optional but, let's face it, you never know when you'll need a little chocolate pick-me-up to brighten the day!

Prep time: 5 minutes • **Total time:** 35 minutes, plus cooling • **Makes:** 12 bars

3 cups (240g) old-fashioned rolled oats

1½ tsp ground cinnamon

¼ tsp ground nutmeg

¼ tsp ground cloves

½ tsp salt

⅓ cup (70g) light or dark brown sugar

½ cup (120ml) pure maple syrup

½ cup (114g) pumpkin purée

1 egg

2 tsp vanilla extract

⅓ cup (45g) pumpkin seeds (AKA pepitas)

⅓ cup (60g) mini chocolate chips

1   Preheat the oven to 350°F (175°C). Line an 8 x 8-in (20 x 20cm) baking pan with aluminum foil and lightly spray with non-stick spray. Set aside.

2   In a large bowl, toss together the oats, cinnamon, nutmeg, cloves, and salt. Set aside. In a medium bowl, whisk the brown sugar and maple syrup together until smooth. Whisk in the pumpkin, then the egg and vanilla. Once thoroughly mixed, pour the wet ingredients into the dry ingredients. Stir with a rubber spatula or large spoon until combined. Fold in the pumpkin seeds and chocolate chips.

3   Spread the mixture into the prepared baking pan and bake for 20 minutes. Allow the bars to cool for 10 minutes at room temperature then transfer to the refrigerator to cool completely. Once chilled, lift the foil out of the pan using the overhang on the sides and slice into bars. The bars will remain fresh in an airtight container at room temperature or in the refrigerator for 7 days. Bars can be frozen for up to 3 months.

SALLY SAYS: Don't like pumpkin seeds? Use chopped pecans or walnuts instead. Want to ditch the chocolate? Try them with butterscotch chips or dried cranberries instead. The bars are highly adaptable for your favorite add-ins.

GLUTEN-FREE

SKINNY BANANA CHOCOLATE CHIP MUFFINS

Healthy or low-fat baked goods have a bad rap. They are known for lacking flavor and moisture, often tasting dry and bland. These bikini-friendly muffins are the complete opposite! In fact, my friends didn't even know they were healthy until I told them. The muffins are sweetened with a touch of honey, brown sugar, and chocolate chips. Because even if you're watching what you eat, there is always room for chocolate!

Prep time: 10 minutes • **Total time:** 30 minutes • **Makes:** 12–14 muffins

2½ cups (310g) white whole wheat flour (or mix of whole wheat and all-purpose flours)

1 tsp baking soda

¼ tsp salt

½ tsp ground cinnamon

¼ cup (85g) honey

½ cup (100g) light brown sugar, loosely packed

2 large ripe bananas, mashed

¼ cup (60g) non-fat yogurt

1 egg, beaten

1 tsp vanilla extract

¾ cup (180ml) milk

¾ cup (135g) chocolate chips

1 banana, thinly sliced, for topping

1 Preheat the oven to 325°F (160°C). Spray a 12-count muffin pan with non-stick spray. Set aside.

2 In a large bowl, gently toss the flour, baking soda, salt, and cinnamon together until combined. Set aside.

3 In a separate bowl, whisk the honey and brown sugar together until relatively smooth. Add the mashed banana, yogurt, beaten egg, and vanilla extract. Slowly pour the wet ingredients into the dry ingredients. Gently begin to fold it all together—it will be very thick. Add the milk slowly and continue to gently mix the ingredients together. The milk will thin everything out, but the batter will still remain thick. Fold in the chocolate chips. Do not overmix the batter.

4 Divide the batter between 12 muffin tins, filling them all the way to the top. If you have leftover batter, bake 1 more batch, filling the empty muffin tins with water to prevent the pan from warping. Top the batter with 2–3 thin slices of the banana. Bake for 17–18 minutes, until very lightly browned on the edges. A toothpick inserted in the center should come out clean. Allow to cool in the pan for 10 minutes. The muffins will remain fresh in an airtight container at room temperature for up to 5 days. Muffins can be frozen up to 3 months.

 SALLY SAYS: The riper your bananas, the more flavor the muffins will have. I buy a bunch of bananas at the beginning of the week and have flavorful banana muffins by the weekend. Don't forget to add those little banana slices on top of the muffins. They seep their moisture inside the muffin as they bake, creating a tender center.

MAPLE PECAN GRANOLA

I have turned granola-haters into granola-lovers with this easy and straightforward recipe. When I gave a few taste-testers this recipe to make, everyone was glad they didn't have to make a trip to the store for the ingredients. All familiar, easy, and common ingredients are used. The sweet maple, spicy cinnamon, and toasted pecans will make you wish for autumn leaves, cozy sweaters, and more granola!

Prep time: 5 minutes • **Total time:** 50 minutes, plus cooling • **Makes:** 2–3 cups

2 cups (160g) old-fashioned oats

½ cup (165g) pure maple syrup

¼ cup (50g) dark brown sugar

¾ cup (105g) chopped pecans

2 tbsp melted coconut or vegetable oil

1 tsp ground cinnamon

pinch salt

1   Preheat the oven to 300°F (145°C). Line a large baking sheet with parchment paper or a silicone baking mat.

2   Combine all the ingredients in a large bowl and stir until all the oats are moistened.

3   Spread onto the prepared baking sheet and bake for 45 minutes, stirring every 15 minutes. Allow to cool completely—the air will help the granola obtain a crunchy texture. Granola remains fresh in an airtight container at room temperature for up to 3 weeks.

 SALLY SAYS: No nuts for you? Try replacing the pecans with dried cranberries, dried cherries, raisins, or pumpkin seeds.

 VEGAN & GLUTEN-FREE

PEANUT BUTTER CHUNK OATMEAL BARS

Close your eyes and think of the most delicious flavor combination out there. I know that you're thinking peanut butter and chocolate—and if you're not, you'll still love this recipe. I first made these healthy oatmeal bars a few years ago after I got sick of paying too much money for store-bought nutrition bars with long lists of unrecognizable ingredients. Each soft bite is loaded with peanut butter, oats, raisins, and chocolate chips. They're a snap to make and give any store-bought snack bar a run for its money!

Prep time: 10 minutes • **Total time:** 30 minutes, plus cooling • **Makes:** 12 bars

½ cup (100g) light brown sugar

1 cup (265g) plus 1 tbsp creamy peanut butter, divided

2 tsp vanilla extract

1 cup (120g) whole wheat flour

1 cup (80g) old-fashioned oats

¼ tsp salt

1 tsp baking soda

½ cup (120ml) milk

¾ cup (135g) mini semi-sweet chocolate chips (or regular size)

½ cup (70g) raisins

1. Preheat the oven to 350°F (175°C). Line the bottom and sides of an 8 x 8-in (20 x 20cm) baking pan with aluminum foil, leaving an overhang on all sides. Set aside.

2. In a large bowl using a handheld or stand mixer fitted with a paddle attachment, beat the brown sugar and 1 cup (265g) of peanut butter on medium speed until light in color and fluffy, about 2 minutes. Mix in the vanilla, scraping down the sides as needed.

3. On low speed, add the flour, oats, salt, and baking soda. The dough will be very thick and clumpy. Slowly add the milk in a steady stream, mixing until a dough forms. With a large spoon or rubber spatula, fold in ½ cup (90g) chocolate chips and raisins.

4. Press the dough lightly into the prepared baking dish. Bake for about 17–20 minutes, until the bars are lightly golden on top. Allow to cool completely. Lift the foil out of the pan using the overhang on the sides and cut into bars.

5. In a small microwave-safe bowl, melt the remaining peanut butter and chocolate chips. Stir until smooth and drizzle over each bar. The bars will remain fresh stored, covered, at room temperature or in the refrigerator for up to 1 week.

 SALLY SAYS: Not a fan of raisins? Use your favorite add-ins instead like nuts, shredded coconut, seeds, dried fruits, or more chocolate chips.

PEANUT BUTTER SWIRL CHOCOLATE SNACK CAKE

Your family and friends will ooh and aah when you treat them to this chocolate and peanut butter cake. Little do they know, it's made with healthier ingredients than most cakes of its kind! In lieu of butter and oil, this cake is left moist from mashed bananas and protein-packed Greek yogurt. Only ½ cup (100g) of sugar sweetens the entire cake, and I managed to squeeze some whole wheat flour in there, too. If you're a fan of peanut butter and chocolate, this cake is your dream come true!

Prep time: 10 minutes • **Total time:** 40 minutes, plus cooling • **Makes:** 12 slices

2 large very ripe bananas, mashed (about 1 cup or 225g)

½ cup (100g) granulated sugar

2 egg whites

¾ cup (180g) Greek yogurt (low-fat or non-fat, vanilla or plain, or regular yogurt)

2 tsp vanilla extract

½ cup (65g) whole-wheat flour

½ cup (60g) all-purpose flour

½ cup (65g) unsweetened cocoa powder

½ tsp salt

1 tsp baking soda

1 tsp baking powder

½ cup (90g) semi-sweet chocolate chips

¼ cup (60g) creamy peanut butter, melted

¼ cup (45g) peanut butter chips (optional)

1 Preheat the oven to 350°F (175°C). Spray an 8 x 8-in (20 x 20cm) baking pan with non-stick spray. Set aside.

2 In a medium bowl, mash the bananas with a fork. Whisk in the granulated sugar, egg whites, yogurt, and vanilla. Set aside.

3 In a large bowl, stir the flours, cocoa powder, salt, baking soda, and baking powder together. Slowly mix in the wet ingredients, being careful not to over-mix. Fold in chocolate chips. The batter will be a little chunky.

4 Pour the batter into the prepared baking pan. Drizzle the melted peanut butter on top and swirl with a knife.

5 Bake for 25–30 minutes, or until a toothpick inserted into the middle comes out clean. Remove the cake from the oven and immediately top with the peanut butter chips. Allow to cool completely before cutting. The cake remains fresh, covered, at room temperature or in the refrigerator for up to 4 days.

 SALLY SAYS: Turn this cake into 12 decadent-tasting cupcakes by baking at 375°F (190°C) for 18–20 minutes.

MOCHA BANANA MILKSHAKE

I'm a self-confessed caffeine junkie. I made this milkshake on a whim one day to switch up my morning cup of Joe. It is worlds tastier than I ever expected! Simply made from a couple frozen bananas, instant coffee, a touch of cocoa, and milk, I can feel good about drinking it, too. The frozen banana chunks are key to its thick and creamy texture. I always keep a bunch of bananas on the counter and once they're turning brown, I chop them up and freeze them for my morning milkshakes.

Prep time: 5 minutes • **Total time:** 5 minutes • **Serves:** 2

3 bananas, peeled, sliced into chunks, and frozen

1 tbsp unsweetened cocoa powder

½ cup (120ml) milk, plus extra (optional)

2 tsp instant coffee

2 tsp vanilla extract

1 Place all of the ingredients into a blender, in the order listed, and blend on high until combined. Scrape down the sides of the blender as needed. Add more milk to thin, if desired. Enjoy immediately.

 SALLY SAYS: Instant coffee is not ground coffee; it has been roasted, ground, brewed, and either spray-dried or freeze-dried. Ground coffee comes from roasted coffee beans and has not been brewed. Instant coffee is found in the coffee aisle.

 VEGAN & GLUTEN-FREE

STRAWBERRY FROZEN YOGURT PIE

There are plenty of pie recipes in this book, but this pink stunner has got to be the easiest. All you need is four ingredients, a pan, and a freezer. That's right, you don't even need an oven! I've made this no-bake pie with all different flavors of frozen yogurt, but simple strawberry is my favorite. Creamy and cool, this lightened up pie hits the spot on a warm summer day.

Prep time: 10 minutes • **Total time:** 6 hours, 10 minutes • **Makes:** 8–12 servings

CRUST

¼ cup (60g) butter, melted

1½ cups (135g) gluten-free graham cracker crumbs (11–12 full-sheet gluten-free graham crackers, see *Sally Says,* right)

FILLING

8oz (226g) container fat-free frozen whipped topping, thawed

1 quart (480g) strawberry frozen yogurt, softened

Light whipped cream and strawberries, to decorate (optional)

1 **MAKE THE CRUST:** Combine the melted butter and Graham cracker crumbs in a medium bowl. Press the mixture evenly into the bottom and up the sides of an 8-in (20cm) springform pan. Set aside.

2 **MAKE THE FILLING:** In a large bowl, stir the frozen whipped topping and frozen yogurt together until softened and combined evenly. Spoon the mixture into the prepared crust. Cover and freeze for about 6 hours or overnight. Garnish with light whipped cream and strawberries, if desired. This pie melts rather quickly, so slice it immediately before serving. The pie may be made 1 day in advance.

 SALLY SAYS: You need to use gluten-free graham crackers if you want this recipe to be truly gluten-free. If you're not gluten-intolerant, however, you can easily swap out the gluten-free version for regular Graham crackers. Either way, they're still delicious!

CHOCOLATE CHERRY ENERGY BITES

One of my favorite snacks to grab before a run are homemade fruit-and-nut bites. I make several variations, but this chocolate-cherry version wins every time. A touch of pure maple syrup gives the bites extra moisture so they stick together when rolled. It also pairs nicely with the tart dried cherries. Made from only a few familiar ingredients, these bites are pure dense energy and their simplicity makes them a perfect on-the-go treat.

Prep time: 10 minutes • **Total time:** 40 minutes • **Makes:** 16 bites

1¾ cups (300g) cashews
(see *Sally Says,* right)

1 cup (120g) dried cherries

2 tsp vanilla extract

2 tbsp unsweetened cocoa powder

1 tbsp pure maple syrup

1   Place all of the ingredients into a blender or food processor, in the order listed, and blend on high for 4–5 minutes, or until a thick and clumpy "dough" is formed. You may have to scrape down the sides of the blender/ food processor a few times to get all of the dry ingredients to the bottom. Once a dough is formed, measure out 2 teaspoons, roll into a ball, and place on a large plate or lined cookie sheet. Repeat with all of the dough.

2   Chill the bites in the refrigerator for at least 30 minutes. Bites stay fresh stored in an airtight container in the refrigerator for up to 7 days.

 SALLY SAYS: I like to use salted, dry-roasted cashews in these bites, but you may use any type of cashew you like best. Cashews may be replaced with almonds or dry-roasted peanuts.

 VEGAN & GLUTEN-FREE

BAKED CINNAMON APPLE CHIPS

These cinnamon spiced apple chips are one of my favorite afternoon snacks. They're crunchy, satisfying, inexpensive, and easy to make. The secret to getting the chips extra crispy is to bake them at a very low temperature for a couple hours. It's also important to use a sharp knife and cut the apple slices very thin. Thick slices will become mushy, not crunchy. Trust me, you will have no problem getting your daily dose of fruit servings with these addicting apple chips!

Prep time: 15 minutes • **Total time:** 3 hours, 15 minutes • **Makes:** 5–6 cups

3 apples, any sweet variety

1 tsp ground cinnamon

1 tbsp granulated sugar

1. Preheat the oven to 200°F (95°C). Line two large baking sheets with parchment paper or silicone baking mats. Set aside.

2. Wash and thinly slice the apples, about 1–2 mm thick. Spread the apple slices over the baking sheets in a single layer. Mix the cinnamon and sugar together in a small bowl. Sprinkle this over the apple slices.

3. Bake for 1 hour, flip the apples over, and bake for 1 more hour. If the apples don't feel crispy, bake for 15 more minutes. Turn the oven off but leave the apples inside as the oven cools down for at least 1 hour—this also helps the slices get crunchy. Tightly cover the chips and store at room temperature for up to 2 weeks.

 Vegan & Gluten-free

INDEX